General Editor: C Vaughan James

ECONOMICS

Christopher St J Yates

ENGLISH LANGUAGE TEACHING

Prentice Hall

New York   London   Toronto   Sydney   Tokyo   Singapore

Published 1992 by
Prentice Hall International (UK) Limited
Campus 400, Maylands Avenue
Hemel Hempstead, Herts HP2 7EZ
a division of
Simon & Schuster International Group

First published 1989 by Cassell Publishers Limited.

A series designed and developed by Passim Ltd, Oxford and Associates

Printed and bound in Great Britain by The Bath Press.

British Library Cataloguing in Publication Data

Information available from the publisher on request.

ISBN 0 13 280256 2

1 2 3 4 5   96 95 94 93 92

CONTENTS

ACKNOWLEDGEMENTS

The passages in this book are taken from BEGG *et al, Economics*, McGraw-Hill, 1984, 1987, to whom the Publisher is grateful for permission to reproduce them.

INTRODUCTION

This course has three purposes. It is intended:
- to introduce you to the **contents** of Economics:
- to provide examples of authentic texts written in the **language** typical of the subject:
- to help you to practise the **skills** you will need in order to study the subject via English and to use it when you have learned it.

No knowledge of Economics is assumed, but if you work through the book carefully you will certainly learn a great deal about it. We do not set out to give comprehensive coverage, but the material does embrace most of the basic concepts. In this sense it is a basic textbook of Economics.

All the texts are taken from a publication about Economics. They are not simplified for learners of English: the language you will encounter in them is exactly what you will meet in real life. We assume that you will have already taken a course of general English and are familiar with the main grammatical structures and much of the vocabulary of everyday use. There may be no such thing as Economics English, but there are a number of words and expressions commonly used in Economics contexts and there are a number of structures also in common use, and these have been isolated for you to practise. So in this sense, this is a textbook of English.

The most important aim of the course, however, is to help you to acquire and develop the skills you will need in order to learn your subject and, when you have finished the course, to use what you will have learned.

When you begin to study a new subject, you do so in two main ways: by **reading** and by **listening**. These are the major means of access to new knowledge and it is on these that we concentrate, via the **book** — for reading, and the **tapes** — for listening. In order to attack all these aims, we have divided each of the 15 units into 8 sections, closely related but each with a slightly different emphasis. Below we give a brief description of each section, so that at any point in any unit you will know exactly what you are expected to do and why you are doing it. The pattern is the same for all units.

A. UNDERSTANDING A PRINTED TEXT (1): In this section you are given a passage to read, usually including a diagram or table, to introduce the topic of the unit. You should first read it through, even if you do not understand it all, looking especially at the way it is set out in paragraphs, with side headings, marginal notes, captions, etc. This will give you a general idea of what it is about and how it is arranged. To help you to identify the most important points in the reading passage, a small number of questions are given, the answers to which you can look out for as you read. You will probably need to read it several times.

B. CHECK YOUR UNDERSTANDING: When you are clear about the general meaning of the passage, you can work through it in more detail with your dictionary. In this section you will be asked to answer a number of detailed questions. You could tackle them by jotting down a few notes and then turning your notes into complete answers, which your teacher will check. You should *always* have a dictionary handy and *never* be too proud (or too lazy!) to look things up.

C. INCREASE YOUR VOCABULARY: In this section you are asked to look at certain words which are used in the text, and there are several kinds of activity to help you remember them. Notice that they are not all new or technical terms; it is often familiar words used in an unfamiliar way that will cause you trouble.

D. CHECK YOUR GRAMMAR: There are probably no new grammatical structures in the texts, but you may need reminding of some of them. The most important ones arising from the texts are revised and practised in this section.

E. UNDERSTANDING A LECTURE / H. UNDERSTANDING DISCOURSE: Sections A–D are all concerned with gaining access to new information through reading, but an important source of information is through listening — to lectures, talks, discussions, even simple conversations between fellow students — so sections E and H are both based on the recordings, to which you should listen (usually several times) before attempting to answer the questions or perform the activities given in your book. You will hear a variety of voices and accents, all speaking at the sort of speed that is customary in an English-speaking environment.

F. UNDERSTANDING A PRINTED TEXT (2) / G. CHECK YOUR UNDERSTANDING: These two sections are very similar to A and B, but the questions in section G are far more detailed and you will need to study the text very carefully in order to answer them.

Although we hope that you will enjoy working through this course, we do not expect you to find it easy. At various times you will probably start wondering how much you have been learning — or your teacher will want to find out what progress you are making. So after Units 5 and 10 we have included progress checks (not tests!) so that you can get a fairly clear idea of this. By the time you have completed Unit 15, you will be ready for anything!

Vaughan James   Oxford, 1989

THREE ECONOMIC ISSUES

A. Understanding a printed text (1)

The following text will introduce you to the topic of **economic issues**. Look at the way it is divided into sections and paragraphs. Pay attention to the headings and notes in the margins, and to the illustration and caption.

Now look at these questions.

1. What is important in the first paragraph?
2. What is the second section about?
3. What is an *oil price shock*?
4. What does the diagram illustrate?
5. What do the oil price shocks show?

Read the passage through and find the answers to the questions. Remember, you do not have to understand every word to answer them.

1-1 THREE ECONOMIC ISSUES

1 Trying to understand what economics is about by studying definitions is like trying to learn to swim by reading an instruction manual. Formal analysis makes sense only once you have some practical experience. In this section we discuss three economic issues to show how society allocates scarce resources between competing uses. In each case we see the importance of the questions what, how, and for whom to produce.

Three important questions

The Oil Price Shocks

2 Oil is an important commodity in modern economies. Oil and its derivatives provide fuel for heating, transport, and machinery, and are basic inputs for the manufacture of industrial petrochemicals and many household products ranging from plastic utensils to polyester clothing. From the beginning of this century until 1973 the use of oil increased steadily. Over much of this period the price of oil fell in comparison with the prices of other products. Economic activity was organized on the assumption of cheap and abundant oil.

Oil used to be cheap

3 In 1973–74 there was an abrupt change. The main oil-producing nations, mostly located in the Middle East but including also Venezuela and Nigeria, belong to OPEC – the Organization of Petroleum Exporting Countries. Recognizing that together they produced most of the world's oil, OPEC decided in 1973 to raise the price for which

Then the price of oil rose

▼

this oil was sold. Although higher prices encourage consumers of oil to try to economize on its use, OPEC correctly forecast that cutbacks in the quantity demanded would be small since most other nations were very dependent on oil and had few commodities available as potential substitutes for oil. Thus OPEC correctly anticipated that a substantial price increase would lead to only a small reduction in sales. It would be very profitable for OPEC members.

Oil price shocks

4   Oil prices are traditionally quoted in US dollars per barrel. Figure 1-1 shows the price of oil from 1970 to 1986. Between 1973 and 1974 the price of oil *tripled*, from $2.90 to $9 per barrel. After a more gradual rise between 1974 and 1978 there was another sharp increase between 1978 and 1980, from $12 to $30 per barrel. The dramatic price increases of 1973–74 and 1978–80 have become known as the OPEC *oil price shocks*, not only because they took the rest of the world by surprise but also because of the upheaval they inflicted on the world economy which had previously been organized on the assumption of cheap oil prices.

People respond to prices

5   Much of this book teaches you that people respond to prices. When the price of some commodity increases, consumers will try to use less of it but producers will want to sell more of it. These responses, guided by prices, are part of the process by which most Western societies determine what, how, and for whom to produce.

The effect of oil price shocks on how the economy produces

6   Consider first *how* the economy produces goods and services. When, as in the 1970s, the price of oil increases sixfold, every firm will try to reduce its use of oil-based products. Chemical firms will develop artificial substitutes for petroleum inputs to their production processes; airlines will look for more fuel-efficient aircraft; electricity will be produced from more coal-fired generators. In general, higher oil prices make the economy produce in a way that uses less oil.

The effect on what is produced

7   How does the oil price increase affect *what* is being produced? Firms and households reduce their use of oil-intensive products which are now more expensive. Households switch to gas-fired central heating and buy smaller cars. Commuters form car-pools or move closer to the city. High prices not only choke off the demand for oil-related commodities; they also encourage consumers to purchase substitute commodities.

Higher demand for these commodities bids up their price and encourages their production. Designers produce smaller cars, architects contemplate solar energy, and research laboratories develop alternatives to petroleum in chemical production. Throughout the economy, what is being produced reflects a shift away from expensive oil-using products towards less oil-intensive substitutes.

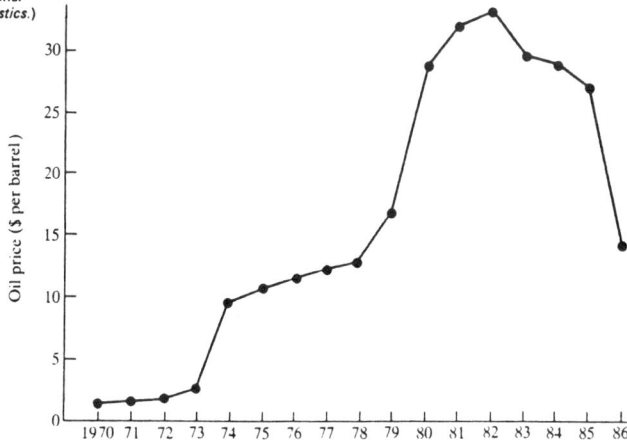

FIGURE 1-1 THE PRICE OF OIL, 1970–86. (Source: IMF, International Financial Statistics.)

8   The *for whom* question in this example has a clear answer. OPEC revenues from oil sales increased from $35 billion in 1973 to nearly $300 billion in 1980. Much of their increased revenue was spent on goods produced in the industrialized Western nations. In contrast, oil-importing nations had to give up more of their own production in exchange for the oil imports that they required. In terms of goods as a whole, the rise in oil prices raised the buying power of OPEC and reduced the buying power of oil-importing countries such as Germany and Japan. The world economy was producing more for OPEC and less for Germany and Japan. Although this is the most important single answer to the 'for whom' question, the economy is an intricate, interconnected system and a disturbance anywhere ripples throughout the entire economy. In answering the 'what' and

The 'for whom' question

The economy is an interconnected system

'how' questions, we have seen that some activities expanded and others contracted following the oil price shocks. Expanding industries may have to pay higher wages to attract the extra labour that they require. For example, in the British economy coal miners were able to use the renewed demand for coal to secure large wage increases. The opposite effects may be expected if the 1986 oil price slump persists.

9   The OPEC oil price shocks example illustrates how society allocates scarce resources between competing uses.

> A *scarce resource* is one for which the demand at a zero price would exceed the available supply.

We can think of oil as having become more scarce in economic terms when its price rose.

A scarce resource

B. Check your understanding

Now read the text carefully, looking up any new items in a dictionary or reference book. Then answer the following questions:

1. What do you need in order to understand economics?

2. What happened to the price of oil from 1900 to 1973?

3. What did OPEC decide in 1973?

4. Why was there only a small reduction in oil sales?

5. What did the oil price shocks lead to?

6. How do people respond to a higher price for a commodity?

7. What effect do higher oil prices have on the economy?

8. What happens throughout the economy when there are high oil prices?

9. What two effects did high prices have on oil-importing countries?

10. When did oil become scarce?

C. Increase your vocabulary

In this section you should use your dictionary to help you answer the questions about the text.

- supply of goods, raw materials etc.
- separation into parts by examination

1. Look at the first paragraph and say which words correspond to these definitions:
- a book which teaches you something
- gives as a share

2. Look at paragraph 2 again and say what words have the opposite meaning to:
- rare, scarce
- outputs
- expensive
- fell, decreased

3. Look at paragraph 3 again and say what words have the same meaning as:
- sudden
- people who used goods or services
- realising
- replacements
- large

4. Look at paragraph 4 again. Can you explain the words:
- quoted
- gradual rise
- sharp increase

5. Look at paragraph 5 again and say what these words refer to:
- line 4: it
- line 5: it

6. Look at paragraph 6 again and say what words have the same meaning as:
- as a rule
- cut down
- six times

7. Look at paragraph 7 again. Can you explain the words:
- household
- commuter
- commodities
- designer
- architect

8. Look at paragraph 8 again and say what words have the opposite meaning to:
- exports
- straightforward
- get, acquire
- didn't need
- getting smaller
- getting larger

9. Look at paragraph 9 again. Can you explain the definition of a scarce resource in your own words?

D. Check your grammar

MAKING STATEMENTS

> **Do you remember?**
> This book *offers* an introduction to economics.
> Economics *is taught* at a great many universities.

1. Use the following verbs to complete the paragraph below:

concern, base, discuss, be, show, take up, be, hope for, say, offer, wish, live, suggest, provide, govern.
Students _____ economics for different reasons. Some _____ a career in business, some _____ for a deeper understanding of government policy, and some _____ about the poor or the unemployed. This book _____ an introduction which _____ that economics _____ a live subject. It _____ real insights into the world in which we _____. The material that we _____ in this book _____ by two ideas. The first _____ that there _____ a body of economics which has to be learned in any introductory course. The second _____ on the belief that modern economics is more readily applicable to the real world than traditional approaches _____.

> **Do you remember?**
> I *passed* my examinations last year.
> He *was accepted* by this univeristy as a student of economics.

2. Now write the following sentences out in full, like this:

Keynes/famous/his/day/economist/own/a/in . . . (be)
Keynes was a famous economist in his own day.

- 1915/Treasury/London/in/he/in/the . . . (join)
- best-known/1935/his/book/in . . . (publish)
- public/war/during/he/service/the/to . . . (recall)
- 5th/in/Cambridge/June/Keynes/1883/on . . . (bear)
- student/he/distinguished/a . . . (be)
- instrumental/the IMF/in/the/1944/World Bank/he/in/and/starting . . . (be)
- Cambridge University/to/1902/he/in . . . (go)
- a/he/as/Cambrdige/teacher/to . . . (return)
- time/he/a/economist/by/as/this/brilliant . . . (accept)
- also/heavy/his/he/by/workload . . . (exhaust)
- *The General Theory of Employment, Interest and Money*/it . . . (call)
- 1919/in/he, with/Treaty of Versailles/he/because/the . . . (resign, disillusion)
- April/on/21st/he/1946 . . . (die)
- book/conventional/this/thinking, enemies/him/many/and (go against, make)

3. Now arrange the sentences you have made into a single paragraph. Make sure that the order you arrange the sentences in makes sense!

E. Understanding a lecture

1. You are now going to hear part of a lecture, divided into sections to help you understand it. As you listen, answer the questions below.

Section 1
- Complete the following statement correctly:
  The lecturer has mentioned three economic issues. In this lecture he is going to talk about
  the first issue ☐
  the second issue ☐
  the third issue ☐
- Note down what the issue is: _____

Section 2
- The lecturer mentions five necessities of life. Note down as many as you can:

  _____

  _____

- Complete the following statement correctly:
  By 'neighbours' the lecturer means
  people living next door to you ☐
  people living in the same town as you ☐
  people living in the same country as you ☐
  people living anywhere in the world ☐

Section 3
Are these statements correct or incorrect? If the answer is correct put a tick ☑ in the box. If it is wrong, put a cross ☒ in the box.
- National income is the money received by the government. ☐
- World income is the total of what every individual in the world earns. ☐

● Fill in the figures the lecturer gives you in the table below.

TABLE 1-1
WORLD POPULATION AND INCOME IN THE EARLY 1980s

	POOR COUNTRIES	MIDDLE-INCOME COUNTRIES	MAJOR OIL COUNTRIES	INDUSTRIAL COUNTRIES	SOVIET BLOC
Income per head (£)					
Percentage of world population					
Percentage of world income					

Source: World Bank, *World Development Report.*

Section 7

● Complete the following statement correctly
  Most of the world's goods are produced for
  poor countries ☐
  middle-income countries ☐
  major oil countries ☐
  industrial countries ☐

Section 8

Are these statements correct or incorrect?
● Workers in poor countries produce less than those in rich countries. ☐
● There is nothing governments can do about the distribution of income. ☐

2. Now wind the cassette back to the beginning of the lecture and listen to it again. This time, instead of answering questions, take notes. The questions you have already answered will help you do this. When you have listened to the whole of the lecture, you will be asked to make a short oral summary of the lecture you have heard. So make sure you note down the most important points of the lecture.

3. You should also write a summary of the lecture, based on your notes.

F. Understanding a printed text (2)

Read the following text carefully, looking up anything you do not understand.

The Role of Government

1 Having mentioned the effect of government tax policy on the income distribution, we now examine in greater detail the role of the government in society. In every society governments provide such services as national defence, police, firefighting services, and the administration of justice. In addition, governments make transfer payments to some members of society.

2   *Transfer payments* are payments made to individuals without requiring the provision of any service in return.

The role of government

Transfer payments

Examples are social security, retirement pensions, unemployment benefits, and, in some countries, food stamps. Government expenditure, whether on the provision of goods and services (defence, police) or on transfer payments, is chiefly financed by imposing taxes, although some (small) residual component may be financed by government borrowing.

A comparison of four countries

3   Table 1-2 compares the role of the government in four countries. In each case, we look at four measures of government spending as a percentage of national income: spending on the direct provision of goods and services for the public, transfer payments, interest on the national debt, and total spending. Italy is a 'big-government' country. Its government spending is large and it needs to raise correspondingly large tax revenues. In contrast, Japan has a much smaller government sector and needs to raise correspondingly less tax revenue. These differences in the scale of government activity relative to national income reflect differences in the way different countries allocate their resources among competing uses.

TABLE 1-2
GOVERNMENT SPENDING AS A PERCENTAGE OF NATIONAL INCOME IN 1985

COUNTRY	PURCHASE OF GOODS AND SERVICES	TRANSFER PAYMENTS	DEBT INTEREST	TOTAL
	%	%	%	%
UK	23.0	17.2	5.1	45.3
Japan	14.9	12.7	4.6	32.2
United States	20.1	12.2	4.8	37.1
Italy	27.0	23.0	9.2	59.4

Source: IMF, *World Economic Outlook, 1986.*

Governments affect what is produced

4   Governments spend part of their revenue on particular goods and services such as tanks, schools, and public safety. They directly affect *what* is produced. Japan's low share of government spending on goods and services in Table 1-2 reflects the very low level of Japanese spending on defence. Governments affect *for whom* output is produced through their tax and transfer payments.

and for whom it is produced

By taxing the rich and making transfers to the poor, the government ensures that the poor are allocated more of what is produced than would otherwise be the case; and the rich get correspondingly less.

and how it is produced

5   The government also affects *how* goods are produced, for example through the regulations it

imposes. Managers of factories and mines must obey safety requirements even where these are costly to implement, firms are prevented from freely polluting the atmosphere and rivers, offices and factories are banned in attractive residential parts of the city.

6   The scale of government activities in the modern economy is highly controversial. In the UK the government takes nearly 40 per cent of national income in taxes. Some governments take a larger share, others a smaller share. Different shares will certainly affect the questions what, how, and for whom, but some people believe that a large government sector makes the economy inefficient, reducing the number of goods that can be produced and eventually allocated to consumers.

7   It is commonly asserted that high tax rates reduce the incentive to work. If half of all we earn goes to the government, we might prefer to work fewer hours a week and spend more time in the garden or watching television. That is one possibility, but there is another one: if workers have in mind a target after-tax income, for example to have at least sufficient to afford a foreign holiday every year, they will have to work *more* hours to meet this target when taxes are higher. Whether on balance high taxes make people work more or less remains an open question. Welfare payments and unemployment benefit are more likely to reduce incentives to work since they actually contribute to target income. If large-scale government activity leads to important disincentive effects, government activity will affect not only what, how, and for whom goods are produced, but also *how much* is produced by the economy as a whole.

8   This discussion of the role of the government is central to the process by which society allocates its scarce resources. It also raises a question. Is it inevitable that the government plays an important role in the process by which society decides how to allocate resources between competing demands? This question lies at the heart of economics, and we return to it shortly when we examine the role of markets in economic life.

9   First, however, we must refine our notion of scarce resources. To do so, we introduce a useful tool of economic analysis, the production possibility frontier.

The question of taxes

The question at the heart of economics

G. Check your understanding

1. Find the terms in the text which describe the following:

- money paid to people without asking for a service in return
- money paid to people when they stop working
- money paid to people who have no work
- money owed by the government of a country
- the money received by governments from taxation
- money a worker keeps after paying taxes

2. Now look at these statements. Using the information in the text, say if they are correct or incorrect.

- Governments do not make free transfer payments. ☐
- Food stamps are an example of a transfer payment. ☐
- Most government income comes from borrowing. ☐
- Japan raises more taxes than Italy. ☐
- Japan spends very little on defence. ☐
- The poor get more of what is produced through taxation and transfer payments. ☐
- Governments do not affect how goods are produced. ☐
- Nobody questions the scale of government economic activity. ☐
- Many people believe that high taxes result in people not wanting to work so hard. ☐
- The production possibility frontier is a tool to examine the role of government in the economy. ☐

3. Now look at paragraph 7 again. Summarise in your own words the arguments for and against high taxes. Then express your own opinion on whether taxes should be high or low.

H. Understanding discourse

1. Listen to this conversation between some students and their tutor. The students should have read the same text that you have just read. The tutor is checking whether they have understood or not. Listen to their tutorial and say whether the students have answered correctly or incorrectly.

If the answer is correct put a tick ☑ in the box. If it is wrong, put a cross ☒ in the box.
1. ☐
2. ☐
3. ☐
4. ☐
5. ☐

2. Did you notice in that conversation how the tutor asked his questions? If you do not understand something, you can ask for an explanation in a number of ways. Look at this table:

(Excuse me) (I'm sorry, but)	can you could you	explain . . . . tell me a bit more about . . .	
	I don't really understand . . . could you (possibly/please) repeat		that last bit . . . what you just said . . .

Imagine you do not understand the following terms. Ask each other for an explanation:
- tax revenue
- unemployment benefit
- retirement pension
- a 'big-government' country
- after-tax income

THE PRODUCTION POSSIBILITY FRONTIER

A. Understanding a printed text (1)

The following text will introduce you to the topic of the **production possibility frontier**. Look at the way it is divided into paragraphs. Pay attention to the heading and notes in the margins, and to the table.

Now look at these questions.

1. What types of good are used as an example?
2. What law is explained?
3. What does Table 1-3 show?
4. When additional workers are added, does output per worker rise or fall?
5. What term is used to describe what happens when society gives up units of food production to get more film output?

Read the passage through and find the answers to the questions. Remember, you do not have to understand every word to answer them.

A hypothetical economy

The law of diminishing returns

THE PRODUCTION POSSIBILITY FRONTIER

1 To see how this tool helps us to think about scarcity and the problem of what to produce, we consider a hypothetical economy in which there are two types of good, food and films. There are four workers in the economy. A worker can produce in either the food industry or the film industry.

2 Table 1-3 shows how much of each good can be produced per week. The answer depends on how the workers are allocated between the two industries. In each industry, the more workers there are, the greater is the total output of the good produced. We have assumed that production in each industry satisfies the *law of diminishing returns*. Each additional worker adds less to total industry output than the previous additional worker added. For example, consider the film industry. Beginning from the position of no workers and no output, the first worker employed increases output by 9 units per week. Adding a

TABLE 1-3			
PRODUCTION POSSIBILITIES IN THE HYPOTHETICAL ECONOMY			
EMPLOYMENT IN FOOD	OUTPUT OF FOOD	EMPLOYMENT IN FILMS	OUTPUT OF FILMS
4	25	0	0
3	22	1	9
2	17	2	17
1	10	3	24
0	0	4	30

second worker raises film output only by 8 units per week, taking total film output to 17 units per week. Adding a third worker increases output by only 7 units per week, and the addition of yet more workers leads to even smaller increases in film output.

3   What lies behind the law of diminishing returns? We have implicitly assumed that workers in the film industry have at their disposal a fixed total amount of cameras, studios, and other equipment. The first worker has sole use of all these facilities. When a second worker is added, the two workers must share these facilities. The addition of further workers reduces equipment per worker to even lower levels. Thus, output per worker in the film industry falls as employment in the film industry rises. One worker produces 9 units per week, two workers average only $8\frac{1}{2}$ units per week, and three workers average only 8 units per week. A similar story applies in the food industry. The fixed total supply of available land, water, and fertilizer must be shared between the total workforce. The first worker, using all these resources, produces 10 units of food per week, but output per person falls to $8\frac{1}{2}$ units per week when two workers share these resources, and is only $7\frac{1}{3}$ units per week when three workers share them. Both industries exhibit diminishing returns as additional workers are added.

The effect on output per worker

Both industries exhibit diminishing returns

4   Table 1-3 shows the possible combinations of food and film output that can be produced in the hypothetical economy if all workers are employed. At one extreme, with all workers employed in food production, the economy can produce 25 units of food and 0 units of film. At the other extreme, with all workers employed in the film industry, the economy can produce 30 units of films but no food. By transferring workers from one industry to the other, the economy can produce more of one good, but only at the expense of producing less of the other good. We say that there is a *trade-off* between food production and film production. In moving down the rows of Table 1-3, society is trading off food for films, giving up units of food production to obtain additional units of film output.

Trade-off

▼

B. Check your understanding

Now read the text carefully, looking up any new items in a dictionary or reference book. Then answer the following questions:

1. What does the production possibility frontier help us to do?

2. What rises when the film industry takes on additional workers?

3. How much does the first worker in the film industry produce?

4. How much does the second worker produce?

5. Why does the first worker in the film industry produce more when on his own?

6. What happens when employment in the film industry rises?

7. Does the same law of diminishing returns apply to food output?

8. How many units of food do three workers produce?

9. What does Table 1-3 assume?

10. What happens to the economy when workers are transferred?

C. Increase your vocabulary

In this section you should use your dictionary to help you answer the questions about the text.

1. Look at the first paragraph and say which words correspond to these definitions:
● based on a suggestion or an idea
● instrument

2. Look at paragraph 2 again and say what words have the same meaning as:
● getting less
● results in
● coming earlier in time order

3. Look at paragraph 3 again. Can you explain the words:
● implicitly
● at their disposal
● equipment
● output
● resources

4. Look at paragraph 4 again and say what words have the same meaning as:
● extra
● moving from . . . to . . .
● get

D. Check your grammar

> **Do you remember?**
> If everyone *has* a job there *is* full employment.
> If more workers *are employed* total output *will increase*.

1. Take one clause from each of the columns below to make one sentence. Make sure your sentences make sense!

- If you don't eat,   you'll see the exit opposite you.
- If you drive carelessly,   consumers will try to use less of it.
- If you don't study   if you pass the exam.
- You'll get run over   if there is high demand.
- If you turn right,   you'll starve.
- If a commodity price goes up,   you'll fail your exam.
- If a price is high,   you won't be able to pay your bills.
- Production is encouraged   you'll have an accident.
- If you spend all your money,   if you cross the road here.
- You'll get a certificate   demand is choked off.

> **Do you remember?**
> If Saudi Arabia *didn't have* oil, it *would not be* so rich.

2. Now say what you think would be the result if the circumstances below actually happened. Complete the sentences, giving your own opinion:

Example:
there/no oil
If there were no oil, we would use other fuels.

- lose/my notes
- economy/collapse
- there/50%/unemployment
- government/halve/taxes
- price/oil/double
- we/stop/use/cars
- I/give/£100,000
- price/food/come down
- I/stop/study/now
- inflation/double
- our currency/lose/all its value

> **Do you remember?**
> If I *had not chosen* economics, I *would have studied* sociology.

3. Use the notes below to make complete sentences on the above model:
- fail/my/entrance exam
- people/not invent/money
- Saudi Arabia/not discover/oil
- I/not come/this university
- government/spend/less/last year

E. Understanding a lecture

1. You are now going to hear part of a lecture, divided into sections to help you understand it. As you listen, answer the questions below.

Section 1
- Note down the tool the lecturer is going to talk about.

Section 2
- Label the diagram below in the way the lecturer tells you to.

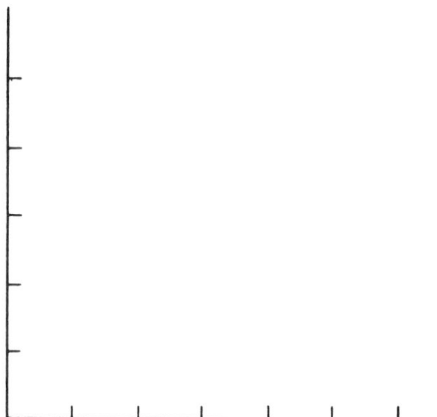

Section 3
- Label the diagram below in the way the lecturer tells you to.

Section 4
- Label the diagram below in the way the lecturer tells you to.

Section 5
- Label the diagram below in the way the lecturer tells you to.

Section 6
- Note down the term the lecturer uses to describe the line you have drawn.

_____

- What is this line called?

_____

- Is this statement correct or incorrect?
  The line shows the maximum combinations that the economy can produce. ☐

Section 7
Are these statements correct or incorrect?
- A movement from B to C means one or more workers have been transferred. ☐
- If we transfer a worker we reduce the total output of film. ☐

2. Now wind the cassette back to the beginning of the lecture and listen to it again. This time, instead of answering questions, take notes. The questions you have already answered will help you do this. When you have listened to the whole of the lecture, you will be asked to give a short oral explanation of the diagram you have drawn. So make sure you note down the most important points of the lecture.

3. You should also write an explanation of the diagram, based on your notes.

F. Understanding a printed text (2)

Read the following text carefully, looking up anything you do not understand.

1   To explain why the curve through the points A to E is called a 'frontier', let us think about the point G in Figure 1-2. Society is then producing 10 units of food and 17 units of films. This is a *feasible* combination. From Table 1-3 it can be seen that this requires one person in the food industry and two in the film industry. But with only three people working, society has spare resources because the fourth person is not being employed. G is *not* a point on the production possibility frontier because it is possible to produce more of one good without sacrificing output of the other good. Putting the extra person to work in the food industry would take us to the point C, yielding 7 extra units of food for the same film output. Putting the extra person to work in the

A feasible combination

G is not on the production possibility frontier

FIGURE 1-2   THE PRODUCTION POSSIBILITY FRONTIER.   The production possibility frontier shows the maximum combinations of output that the economy can produce using all available resources. The frontier represents a trade-off; more of one commodity implies less of the other. Points such as *H* lying above the frontier are unattainable. They require more resource inputs than the economy has available. Points such as *G* inside the frontier are inefficient. By fully utilizing available resource inputs the economy could expand output and produce on the frontier.

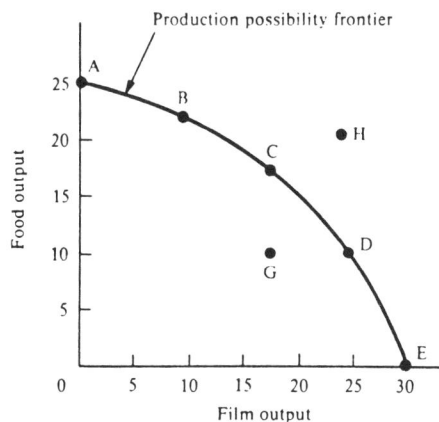

film industry would take us to the point *D*, with 7 extra units of films but no loss of food output.

2 The production possibility frontier shows the points at which society is producing *efficiently*. More output of one good can be obtained only by sacrificing output of the other good. Points such as *G*, which lie inside the frontier, are *inefficient* because society is wasting resources. More output of one good would not require less output of the other. In our hypothetical example, the waste or inefficiency arises because some members of the potential workforce are not being used to produce goods.

3 Points that lie outside the production possibility frontier, such as the point *H* in Figure 1-2, are said to be *unattainable*. It would be nice to have even more food and films but, given the amount of labour available, it is simply impossible to produce this output combination. Scarcity of resources, in this example the restriction that at most only four workers are available for producing goods, limits society to a choice of points that lie inside or on the production possibility frontier. Society has to accept that its resources are scarce and make choices about how to allocate these scarce resources between competing uses. In this example, the competing uses are employment in the food industry and employment in the film industry.

4 Given that people like food and films, society should want to produce efficiently. To select a point inside the production possibility frontier is to sacrifice output unnecessarily. Society's problem is therefore to make a choice between the different points that lie on the production possibility frontier. In so doing, it decides *what* to produce. It might select the point *A*, with no films but a lot of food, or the point *C*, with a more balanced mixture of food and films. Depending on society's preferences between food and films, it might choose any point on the production possibility frontier. However, in choosing a particular point, society will also be choosing *how* to produce. It will then be necessary to refer back to Table 1-3 to determine how many workers must be allocated to each of the industries to produce the desired output combination. As yet, our example is too simple to show *for whom* society produces. To answer that question, we need more information than the position on the production possibility frontier.

Efficient production

Inefficient production

Unattainable points

Society must choose how to allocate its scarce resources

Society's problem

What society decides

▼

G. Check your understanding

Are these statements correct or incorrect?

- At point G society has spare resources. ☐
- G is not on the production possibility frontier because one worker is employed in another industry. ☐
- If the extra person joins the film industry food output will go down. ☐
- Point G is feasible but not efficient. ☐
- Point H is a point which cannot be achieved. ☐
- Point H is unattainable because there are not enough workers. ☐
- Society must choose between inefficient and unattainable points. ☐
- Society can choose to produce at any point on the frontier. ☐
- Society's choice of point on the frontier does not affect how it produces. ☐
- The example the writer has given can easily answer the question 'for whom' society produces. ☐

H. Understanding discourse

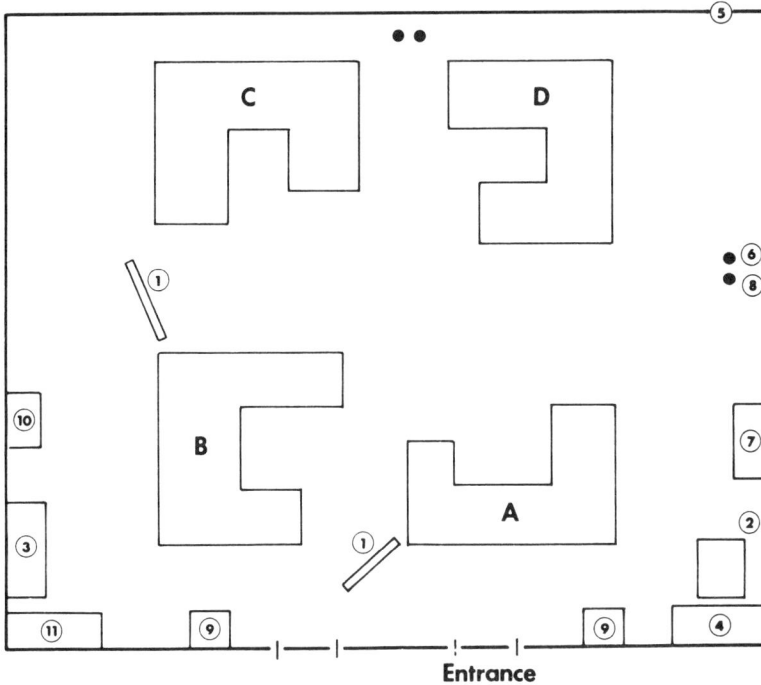

You want to find:
- dictionaries ☐
- reference books ☐
- magazines ☐
- newspapers ☐
- books on macroeconomics ☐
- books on microeconomics ☐
- World Bank reports ☐
- International Monetary Fund bulletins ☐
- government statistics ☐

3

MARKETS

A. Understanding a printed text (1)

The following text will introduce you to the topic of **markets**. Look at the way it is divided into paragraphs. Pay attention to the heading and the notes in the margins.

Now look at these questions:

1. From the heading, what do you expect the text to be about?

2. What does paragraph 2 give you?

3. What example does the writer give to illustrate markets and prices?

4. What decides you to buy a hamburger?

5. What does the writer's definition of markets emphasise?

Read the passage through and find the answers to the questions. Remember, you do not have to understand every word to answer them.

1-3 THE ROLE OF THE MARKET

1 Markets bring together buyers and sellers of goods and services. In some cases, such as a local fruit stall, buyers and sellers meet physically. In other cases, such as the stock market, business can be transacted over the telephone, almost by remote control. We need not go into these details. Instead, we use a general definition of markets.

What the term market means

2 A *market* is a shorthand expression for the process by which households' decisions about consumption of alternative goods, firms' decisions about what and how to produce, and workers' decisions about how much and for whom to work are all reconciled by adjustment of *prices*.

3 Prices of goods and of resources, such as labour, machinery and land, adjust to ensure that scarce resources are used to produce those goods and services that society demands.

Economics studies markets and prices

4 Much of economics is devoted to the study of how markets and prices enable society to solve the problems of what, how, and for whom to produce. Suppose you buy a hamburger for your lunch. What does this have to do with markets and prices? You chose the café because it was fast, convenient and cheap. Given your desire to eat, and your limited resources, the low hamburger price told you that this was a good way to satisfy your appetite. You probably prefer steak but that is more expensive. The price of steak is high enough to ensure that society answers the 'for whom' question about lunchtime steaks in favour of someone else.

5   Now think about the seller's viewpoint. The café owner is in the business because, given the price of hamburger meat, the rent and the wages that must be paid, it is still possible to sell hamburgers at a profit. If rents were higher, it might be more profitable to sell hamburgers in a cheaper area or to switch to luxury lunches for rich executives on expense accounts. The student behind the counter is working there because it is a suitable part-time job which pays a bit of money. If the wage were much lower it would hardly be worth working at all. Conversely, the job is unskilled and there are plenty of students looking for such work, so owners of cafés do not have to offer very high wages.

6   Prices are guiding your decision to buy a hamburger, the owner's decision to sell hamburgers, and the student's decision to take the job. Society is allocating resources – meat, buildings, and labour – into hamburger production through the price system. If nobody liked hamburgers, the owner could not sell enough at a price that covered the cost of running the café and society would devote no resources to hamburger production. People's desire to eat hamburgers guides resources into hamburger production. However, if cattle contracted a disease, thereby reducing the economy's ability to produce meat products, competition to purchase more scarce supplies of beef would bid up the price of beef, hamburger producers would be forced to raise prices, and consumers would buy more cheese sandwiches for lunch. Adjustments in prices would encourage society to reallocate resources to reflect the increased scarcity of cattle.

7   There were several markets involved in your purchase of a hamburger. You and the café owner were part of the market for lunches. The student behind the counter was part of the local labour market. The café owner was part of the local wholesale meat market and the local market for rented buildings. These descriptions of markets are not very precise. Were you part of the market for lunches, the market for prepared food, or the market for sandwiches to which you would have turned if hamburgers had been more expensive? That is why we have adopted a very general definition of markets which emphasizes that they are arrangements through which prices influence the allocation of scarce resources.

▼

B. Check your understanding

Now read the text carefully, looking up any new items in a dictionary or reference book. Then answer the following questions:

1. What example is given of a market where sellers and buyers actually meet?

2. How are households' decisions on what to buy reconciled?

3. Why do prices adjust?

4. What problems do markets and prices solve for society?

5. Why is the café owner in business?

6. Why do café owners not have to pay high wages?

7. What makes society put resources into hamburger production?

8. What would consumers do if hamburger prices rose?

9. How many markets does the writer say you are involved in if you buy a hamburger?

10. Does the writer give an exact description of a market?

C. Increase your vocabulary

In this section you should use your dictionary to help you answer the questions about the text.

1. Look at the first paragraph and say what words have the same meaning as:
- at a distance
- of the neighbourhood
- carried out, done

2. Look at paragraph 2 again. Can you explain in your own words the writer's definition of markets?

3. Look at paragraph 3 again and say what words have the same meaning as:
- ask for
- make certain that

4. Using words from paragraph 4, can you complete the following statements?
- I quite like lamb but really I . . . . beef.
- He was a very keen student. He . . . . most of his time to his studies.
- I don't like the canteen, but it's more . . . . than going out to a café.
- I'm not in . . . . of long and expensive lunches.

- Please . . . . that your essays reach me on time.
- A good degree should . . . . you to get a job.

5. Look at paragraph 5 again. Can you explain the words:
- rent
- profit
- expense account
- part-time job

6. Look at paragraph 6 again and say what words have the same meaning as:
- buy
- illness
- managing
- put up
- rareness

7. Look at paragraph 7 again. Can you explain the words:
- labour market
- wholesale (meat) market

D. Check your grammar

> **Do you remember?**
> Some verbs in English are followed by the infinitive, 'to':
>   She *wants to leave* early today.
>
> Others are followed by the -ing form:
>   He *enjoys playing* any kind of sport.
>
> Some verbs can take both 'to' and -ing, but their meaning sometimes changes:
>
>   He *remembered* (= did not forget) *to book* a table.
>   I *remember* (= recall) *seeing* that film about five years ago.

1. Complete the following sentences:
* He suggested (go) . . . . into the country on Sunday.
* I'm sorry I forgot (return) . . . . your book yesterday.
* Stop (make) . . . . that noise! I can't work.
* Which definition would you use (describe) . . . . markets?
* You must avoid (make) . . . . unnecessary mistakes.
* Try (understand) . . . . the difference between microeconomics and macroeconomics.
* Try (pay) . . . . more attention to what I say.
* Would you mind (lend) . . . . me your notes?
* Tomorrow I intend (discuss) . . . . macroeconomics with you.
* Serious illness prevented him from (take) . . . . the exam.
* I am looking forward to (study) . . . . economics.

2. Match the following clauses together, using *and, but, when, after, so* and *because*:

I worked hard all week	I wanted some company
my friend was driving home	we drive into the country
a long argument	I decided to get away on Sunday
I invited a friend to go with me	we were involved in an accident
they said it wasn't his fault	the other driver didn't agree
it wasn't his fault	we called the police
we hired a car for the day	it was an unpleasant end to the day.

3. Now arrange your sentences into a sensible paragraph.

E. Understanding a lecture

You are now going to hear part of a lecture, divided into short sections to help you understand it. As you listen, answer the questions below.

Section 1
Complete the following statement with the words the lecturer uses:

* Markets are _____ through which prices influence how we _____ _____.
* Note down how many kinds of economy the lecturer is going to talk about.

Section 2
- Note down the first kind of economy.

_____

- Is this statement correct or incorrect?
  In this kind of economy the government decides what should be produced and what
  should be consumed. ☐

Section 3
- Is this statement correct or incorrect?
  To plan this kind of economy is very simple. ☐
- Note down the country that is an example of this kind of economy.

_____

- Is this statement correct or incorrect?
  In this kind of economy the government does not own factories or land. ☐

Section 4
- Note down the kind of economy the lecturer is talking about.

_____

- Is this statement correct or incorrect?
  You cannot become a millionaire in this kind of economy. ☐
- Note down the country that is an example of this kind of economy.

_____

Section 5
- Note down the kind of economy the lecturer is talking about.

_____

- Which two sections of society interact in this kind of economy?

_____

- Is this statement correct or incorrect?
  Most countries have economies of this kind. ☐

2. Now wind the cassette back to the beginning of the lecture and listen to it again. This
time, instead of answering questions, take notes. The questions you have already answered
will help you do this. When you have listened to the whole of the lecture, you will be asked
to give a short oral summary of it. So make sure you note down the most important points of
the lecture.

3. You should also write a summary of the lecture, based on your notes.

F. Understanding a printed text (2)

Read the following text carefully, looking up anything you do not understand.

1-4 POSITIVE AND NORMATIVE ECONOMICS

1 In studying economics it is important to distinguish two branches of the subject. The first is known as 'positive economics', the second as 'normative economics'.

> *Positive economics* deals with objective or scientific explanations of the working of the economy.

The aim of positive economics is to explain how society makes decisions about consumption, production, and exchange of goods. The purpose of this investigation is twofold: to satisfy our curiosity about why the economy works as it does, and to have some basis for predicting how the economy will respond to changes in circumstances. Normative economics is very different.

> *Normative economics* offers prescriptions or recommendations based on personal value judgements.

In positive economics, we hope to act as detached scientists. Whatever our political persuasion, whatever our view about what we would like to happen or what we would regard as 'a good thing', in the first instance we have to be concerned with how the world actually works. At this stage, there is no scope for personal value judgements. We are concerned with propositions of the form: if *this* is changed then *that* will happen. In this regard, positive economics is similar to the natural sciences such as physics, geology, or astronomy.

2 Here are some examples of positive economics in action. Economists of widely differing political persuasions would agree that, when the government imposes a tax on a good, the price of that

Positive economics

Normative economics

Some examples of positive economics

▼

good will rise. The normative question of whether this price rise is desirable is entirely distinct. Similarly, there would be substantial agreement that the following proposition of positive economics is correct: favourable weather conditions will increase wheat output, reduce the price of wheat, and increase the consumption of wheat. Many propositions in positive economics would command widespread agreement among professional economists.

Disagreements

3   Of course, as in any other science, there are unresolved questions where disagreement remains. These disagreements are at the frontiers of economics. Research in progress will resolve some of these issues but new issues will arise and provide scope for further research.

4   Although competent and comprehensive research can in principle resolve many of the outstanding issues in positive economics, no corresponding claim can be made about the resolution of disagreement in normative economics. Normative economics is based on subjective value judgements, not on the search for any objective truth. The following statement combines positive and normative economics: 'The elderly have very high medical expenses compared with the rest of the population, and the government should subsidize health bills of the aged.' The first part of the proposition – the claim that the aged have relatively high medical bills – is a statement in positive economics. It is a statement about how the world works, and we can imagine a research programme that could determine whether or not it is correct. Broadly speaking, this assertion happens to be correct. The second part of the proposition – the recommendation about what the government should do – could never be 'proved' to be correct or false by any scientific research investigation. It is simply a subjective value judgement based on the feelings of the person making the statement. Many people might happen to share this subjective judgement, for example those people who believe that all citizens alive today should be able to purchase roughly equal amounts of luxury and recreational goods after paying for the necessities of life. But other

The basis of normative economics

A combination of positive and normative economics

people might reasonably disagree. You might believe that it is more important to devote society's scarce resources to improving the environment.

5   There is no way that economics can be used to show that one of these normative judgements is correct and the other is wrong. It all depends on the preferences or priorities of the individual or the society that has to make this choice. But that does not mean that economics can throw no light on normative issues. We can use positive economics to spell out the detailed implications of making the choice one way or the other. For example, we might be able to show that failure to subsidize the medical bills of the elderly leads middle-aged people to seek a lot of unnecessary medical check-ups in an attempt to detect diseases before their treatment becomes expensive. Society might have to devote a great deal of resources to providing check-up facilities, leaving less resources available than had been supposed to devote to improving the environment. Positive economics can be used to clarify the menu of options from which society must eventually make its normative choice.

Economics can neither prove nor disprove normative judgements

The use of positive economics

G. Check your understanding

1. Look at the first paragraph again.
Is this statement correct or incorrect?
● Normative economics is based on personal opinion, whereas positive economics is
   objective.   ☐

Say which words have the opposite meaning to:
● subjective
● lack of interest
● treat as the same
● involved

Can you explain the words:
● predicting
● personal value judgement
● proposition

2. Look at paragraph 2 again and say what words have the same meaning as:
● completely
● found over a large area
● places . . . on
● large, considerable

3. Look at paragraph 3 again and say what words have the same meaning as:
- come up
- provide a solution

4. Look at paragraph 4 again. Are these statements correct or incorrect?
- Research cannot bring about agreement in normative economics. ☐
- Positive economics is a search for objective truth. ☐
- The statement 'the government should subsidise health bills of the aged' belongs within the field of normative economics. ☐
- Research cannot prove whether this statement is right or wrong. ☐

5. Look at paragraph 5 again and say what words have the opposite meaning to:
- not to notice or see
- success
- confuse
- general
- things with no claim to consideration

H. Understanding discourse

A lecturer is giving the title for an essay to be written during the coming week. He is also giving the main points that must be covered. Listen to what he says and note down what you must do.

_____

_____

_____

_____

_____

_____

MICROECONOMICS AND MACROECONOMICS

A. Understanding a printed text (1)

The following text will introduce you to the topic of **microeconomics and macroeconomics**. Look at the way it is divided into paragraphs. Pay attention to the notes in the margin.

Now look at these questions:

1. How are the different branches of economics classified?
2. What does microeconomics do?

3. Is the general equilibrium theory part of microeconomics or macroeconomics?
4. Is partial analysis part of microeconomics or macroeconomics?
5. What does macroeconmics do?

Read the passage through and find the answers to these questions. Remember, you do not have to understand every word to answer them.

1-5 MICROECONOMICS AND MACROECONOMICS

1 Many economists specialize in a particular branch of the subject. For example, there are labour economists, energy economists, monetary economists, and international economists. What distinguishes these economists is the segment of economic life in which they are interested. Labour economics deals with problems of the labour market as viewed by firms, workers, and society as a whole. Urban economics deals with city problems: land use, transport, congestion, and housing. However, we need not classify branches of economics according to the area of economic life in which we ask the standard questions what, how, and for whom. We can also classify branches of economics according to the approach or methodology that is used. The very broad division of approaches into microeconomic and macroeconomic cuts across the large number of subject groupings cited above.

Microeconomic analysis offers a detailed treatment of individual decisions about particular commodities.

For example, we might study why individual households prefer cars to bicycles and how producers decide whether to produce cars or bicycles. We can then aggregate the behaviour of all households and all firms to discuss total car purchases and total car production. Within a

Economists specialise

How economics can be classified

Microeconomics

market economy we can discuss the market for cars. Comparing this with the market for bicycles, we may be able to explain the relative price of cars and bicycles and the relative output of these two goods. The sophisticated branch of microeconomics known as *general equilibrium theory* extends this approach to its logical conclusion. It studies simultaneously every market for every commodity. From this it is hoped that we can understand the complete pattern of consumption, production, and exchange in the whole economy at a point in time.

General equilibrium theory

2   If you think this sounds very complicated you are correct. It is. For many purposes, the analysis becomes so complicated that we tend to lose track of the phenomena in which we were interested. The interesting task for economics, a task that retains an element of art in economic science, is to devise judicious simplifications which keep the analysis manageable without distorting reality too much. It is here that microeconomists and macroeconomists proceed down different avenues. Microeconomists tend to offer a detailed treatment of one aspect of economic behaviour but ignore interactions with the rest of the economy in order to preserve the simplicity of the analysis. A microeconomic analysis of miners' wages would emphasize the characteristics of miners and the ability of mine owners to pay. It would largely neglect the chain of indirect effects to which a rise in miners' wages might give rise. For example, car workers might use the precedent of the miners' pay increase to secure higher wages in the car industry, thus being able to afford larger houses which burned more coal in heating systems. When microeconomic analysis ignores such indirectly induced effects it is said to be *partial analysis*.

Economics needs simplifications

Indirect effects lead to partial analysis

3   In some instances, indirect effects may not be too important and it will make sense for economists to devote their effort to very detailed analyses of particular industries or activities. In other circumstances, the indirect effects are too important to be swept under the carpet and an alternative simplification must be found.

Macroeconomics

    Macroeconomics emphasizes the interactions in the economy as a whole. It deliberately simplifies the individual building blocks of the analysis in order to retain a manageable analysis of the complete interaction of the economy.

For example, macroeconomists typically do not worry about the breakdown of consumer goods into cars, bicycles, televisions, and calculators. They prefer to treat them all as a single bundle called 'consumer goods' because they are more interested in studying the interaction between households' purchases of consumer goods and firms' decisions about purchases of machinery and buildings.

B. Check your understanding

Now read the text carefully, looking up any new items in a dictionary or reference book. Then answer the following questions:

1. What distinguishes an energy economist from an urban economist?

2. Are the same questions asked in each area of economic life?

3. What is needed before total car purchases and production can be discussed?

4. What does the general equilibrium theory examine?

5. What can be understood from such a study?

6. What happens when an analysis becomes too complicated?

7. What can keep an analysis manageable?

8. What do most microeconomists leave out of their analysis?

9. What does partial analysis ignore?

10. Why would most macroeconomists not make a breakdown of consumer goods?

C. Increase your vocabulary

In this section you should use a dictionary to help you answer the questions about the text.

1. Look at the first paragraph again. What words correspond to these definitions?
- way of studying a subject
- give particular attention to
- way of looking at a subject
- quoted

2. Look at the first paragraph again and say what words have the opposite meaning to:
- beginning
- at different times
- simple and uncomplicated

3. Look at the first paragraph again. Can you explain the words:
- consumption
- exchange

4. Look at paragraph 2 and say which words have the same meaning as:
- pulling out of shape
- pay not enough attention to
- pay no attention to
- think out, plan

- keep safe
- brought about
- showing or having good sense

5. Look at paragraph 3 and say which words have the same meaning as:
- keep
- makes easier, less complicated
- as a rule, characteristically
- be sensible

D. Check your grammar

DEFINING

> **Do you remember?**
> A labour economist is a person *who* deals with problems of the labour market.
>
> The segment of economic life in *which* I am most interested is urban economics.

1. Define each of the words given below. Use the examples above as a model.
- an energy economist is . . .
- international economics
- a monetary economist
- baseball
- consumer goods
- microeconomics
- macroeconomics
- a worker
- a miner
- coal

ADJECTIVES AND ADVERBS

> **Do you remember?**
> General equilibrium theory is a *relatively difficult* branch of economics to understand.
>
> That looks an *expensive* cassette player.
> Actually, I bought it quite *cheaply*.

2. Complete the following sentences, using the words in brackets.
- This is a . . . . book to read.
  (comparative, easy).

- . . . . car production is not always . . . . to estimate . . . .
  (total, easy, accurate)

- Even some . . . . tools of . . . . analysis are not . . . . known.
  (common, economic, general)

- Some microeconomic analyses offer . . . . detailed treatments of . . . .
  decisions.
  (extreme, individual)

- If we compare the market for cars and bicycles . . . . , we may be able to offer
  a . . . . explanation for their . . . . prices.
  (careful, good, relative)

- .... she managed to pass her .... exams ....
  (fortunate, final, easy)

- My tutor emphasised the .... importance of putting ideas in a .... order.
  (great, logical)

- .... analysis ignores .... induced effects.
  (partial, indirect)

- The .... economist keeps his analysis .... without .... distorting reality.
  (sensible, manageable, undue)

- She's an .... novelist – something .... and ....
  happens in her stories.
  (excellent, unusual, exciting, constant)

E. Understanding a lecture

You are now going to hear part of a lecture, divided into short sections to help you understand it. As you listen, answer the questions below.

Section 1
Are these statements correct or incorrect?
- The students will not study macroeconomics at all after this lecture. ☐
- The lecturer expects his students to have heard more about macroeconomics than microeconomics. ☐
- Macroeconomics is of greater public interest than microeconomics. ☐

Section 2
- How many key terms is the lecturer going to talk about?

  _____

- Note down the first term the lecturer introduces.

  _____

- Note down the abbreviation for this term.

  _____

- Note down the meaning of the term.

  _____

  _____

Section 3
- Note down the next term the lecturer introduces.

  _____

- Note down the meaning of the term.

  _____

  _____

- Is this statement correct or incorrect?
  Prices of different goods move in line with each other. ☐
- Note down the term the lecturer uses to describe an economy in which the price level is rising.

_____

Section 4————————————————————————————————

- Note down the next term the lecturer introduces.

_____

- Note down the meaning of the term.

_____

_____

- Is this statement correct or incorrect?
  The labour force includes those people who don't have to work but are of working age. ☐

2. Now wind the cassette back to the beginning of the lecture and listen to it again. This time, instead of answering questions, take notes. The questions you have already answered will help you do this. When you have listened to the whole of the lecture, you will be asked to give a short oral summary of it. So make sure you note down the most important points of the lecture.

3. You should also write a summary of the lecture, based on your notes.

F. Understanding a printed text (2)

The following text provides a summary of what you have read about and listened to so far. Read the text carefully, looking up anything you do not understand.

SUMMARY

1   Economics analyses what, how, and for whom society produces. The central economic problem is to reconcile the conflict between people's virtually unlimited demands with society's limited ability to produce goods and services to fulfil these demands.

2   The production possibility frontier shows the maximum amount of one good that can be produced for each given level of output of the other good. It depicts the trade-off or menu of choices that society must make in deciding what to produce. Resources are scarce and points outside the frontier are unattainable. It is inefficient to produce within the frontier. By moving on to the frontier, society could have more of some good without having less of any other good.

3   Industrial Western countries rely extensively on markets to allocate resources. The market is the process by which production and consumption decisions are co-ordinated through adjustments in prices. The role of prices is central to this definition.

4   In a command economy, decisions on what, how, and for whom are made in a central planning office. No economy relies entirely on command, but there is extensive planning in many Soviet bloc countries.

5   A free market economy has no government intervention. Resources are allocated entirely through markets in which individuals pursue their own self-interest.

6   Modern economies in the West are mixed, relying mainly on the market but with a large dose of government intervention. The optimal level of government intervention remains a subject of controversy.

7   Positive economics studies how the economy actually behaves. Normative economics makes prescriptions about what should be done. The two should be kept separate as far as possible. Given sufficient research, economists should eventually agree on issues in positive economics. Normative economics involves subjective value judgements. There is no reason why economists should agree about normative statements.

8   Microeconomics offers a detailed analysis of particular activities in the economy. For simplicity, it may neglect some interactions with the rest of the economy. Macroeconomics emphasizes these interactions at the cost of simplifying the individual building blocks.

G. Check your understanding

1. Look at the first paragraph again. What words have the same meaning as:
- almost
- in the middle
- argument, disagreement

2. Look at paragraph 2 again. What words have the opposite meaning to:
- can be achieved
- working well

3. Look at paragraph 3 again. What words have the same meaning as:
- depend on
- brought together

4. Look at paragraph 4 again. What word has the opposite meaning to:
- a small amount of

5. Look at paragraph 5 again. What does this word refer to?
- line 2: in which

▼

6. Look at paragraph 6 again. What words have the same meaning as:
- disagreement
- for the most part
- stays

7. Look at paragraph 7 again. What words have the opposite meaning to:
- together
- not enough

8. Look at paragraph 8 again. What words have the same meaning as:
- making less complicated
- pay little or no attention to

9. Now look at these key terms. Write a short explanation of each one. You can refer back to previous units if you want.

Scarcity

_____

_____

Income distribution

_____

_____

Transfer payments

_____

_____

Production possibility frontier

_____

_____

Diminishing returns

_____

_____

The free market

_____

_____

The command economy

_____

_____

The mixed economy

_____

_____

Microeconomics

_____

_____

Macroeconomics

_____

_____

Gross national product   .

_____

_____

Inflation

_____

_____

Unemployment rate

_____

_____

H. Understanding discourse

Listen to this lecturer explaining what you must do if there is a fire in the building. You are in room 101. If there was a fire now, where would you go?

_____

_____

A. Understanding a printed text (1)

The following text will introduce you to the topic of **economic analysis**. Look at the way it is divided into paragraphs. Pay attention to the notes in the margin.

Now look at these questions:

1. What is the overall purpose of this chapter?
2. What does a model do?
3. In how many ways does data interact with models?
4. Why is the word *relevant* important?
5. How is the writer going to introduce the tools of economic analysis?

Read the passage through and find the answers. Remember, you do not have to understand every word to answer them.

THE TOOLS OF ECONOMIC ANALYSIS

Positive and normative economics

1 Positive economics analyses issues relating to the description of the past and the prediction of the future. It tries to explain why the oil price shock led to a switch to smaller cars and whether this trend will continue. Normative economics analyses issues relating to society's value judgements. Should society try to conserve scarce and expensive oil by raising the tax on petrol even though this will penalize car users still further?

2   In this chapter the emphasis is not on learning economics but on mastering the tools of the trade. To analyse economic issues we use both *models* and *data*.

What a model does

A *model* or theory makes a series of simplifying assumptions from which it deduces how people will behave. It is a deliberate simplification of reality.

What a model is

Models are frameworks for organizing the way we think about a problem. They simplify by omitting some details of the real world to concentrate on the essentials. From this manageable picture of reality we develop our analysis of how the economy works.

How an economist uses a model

3   An economist uses a model in the way a traveller uses a map. A map of London misses out many features of the real world – traffic lights, roundabouts, the exact width of streets – but if you study it carefully you can get a good picture of how the traffic is likely to flow and what will be the best route to take. This simplified picture is easy to follow, yet helps you understand real-world behaviour when you must drive through the city in the rush hour.

How the tools of the trade will be introduced

4   The data or facts interact with models in two ways. First, the data help us quantify the relationships to which our theoretical models draw attention. It may be insufficient to work out that all bridges across the Thames are likely to be congested. To choose the best route we need to know how long we would have to queue at each bridge. We need some facts. The model is useful because it tells us which facts are likely to be the most important. Bridges are more likely to be congested than six-lane motorways.

5   Second, the data help us to *test* our models. Like all careful scientists, economists must check that their theories square with the relevant facts. Here the crucial word is *relevant*. It is this that prevents a chimpanzee or a computer sifting through all the facts in the world to establish the single definitively correct theory. For example, it turns out that the number of Scottish dysentery deaths is closely related to the actual inflation rate in the UK over many decades. Is this a factual coincidence or the key to a theory of inflation in the UK? The facts alert us to the need to ponder this question, but we can make a decision only by recourse to logical reasoning.

Decisions are made by logical reasoning

6   In this instance, since we can find no theoretical or logical connection, we regard the close factual relationship between Scottish dysentery deaths and UK inflation as a coincidence that should be ignored. Without any logical underpinning, the empirical connection will break down sooner or later. Paying attention to this spurious relationship in the data neither increases our understanding of the economy nor increases our confidence in predicting the future.

7   The blend of models and data is thus a subtle one. The data may alert us to logical relationships we had previously overlooked. And whatever theory we wish to maintain should certainly be checked against the facts. But only theoretical reasoning can guide an intelligent assessment of what evidence should be regarded as being of reasonable relevance.

8   To introduce the tools of the trade we begin with the representation of economic data in tables, charts, and figures (diagrams). Then we show how an economist might approach the development of a theoretical model of an economic relationship. Finally, we discuss how actual data might be used to test the theory that has been developed.

How data interact with models

▼

B. Check your understanding

Now read the text carefully, looking up any new items in a dictionary or reference book. Then answer the following questions:

1. What does positive economics analyse?

2. What does normative economics analyse?

3. What tools are used to analyse economic issues?

4. What do models leave out?

5. To what does the writer compare a model?

6. What is the first way in which data interact with models?

7. What is the second way in which data interact with models?

8. How does the economist decide whether Scottish dysentery deaths are related to the UK inflation rate?

9. Is there any relationship between Scottish dysentery deaths and the UK inflation rate?

10. What are the second and third parts of the chapter going to be about?

C. Increase your vocabulary

1. Look at the first paragraph again. What words have the same meaning as:
- keep from use
- something said before it happens
- change from one thing to another

2. Look at paragraph 2 again and explain what the following mean:
- tools of the trade
- data
- frameworks

3. Look at paragraph 3 again. What words have the opposite meaning to:
- includes
- improbable
- imprecise

4. Look at paragraph 4 again and say what these words refer to:
- line 3: to which
- line 7: it

5. Look at paragraph 5 again. What words have the same meaning as:
- correspond to, are in line with
- tens of years
- think carefully about
- most important
- put on a firm foundation
- give warning

6. Look at paragraph 6 again. What words have the same meaning as:
- trust
- false
- relying on observation

7. Look at paragraph 7 again. What words have the opposite meaning to:
- afterwards
- crude
- stupid

8. Look at paragraph 8 again and explain what the following mean:
- tables
- charts
- diagrams

D. Check your grammar

> **Do you remember?**
> That lecture *hasn't taken place* yet. It's tomorrow.
> The seminar *has already been given*. It took place yesterday.

1. Look at this timetable for the Economics department at a university. The time now is 6 o'clock on the Wednesday evening. Say what has already happened and what has not happened yet.

	MONDAY	TUESDAY	WEDNESDAY	THURSDAY	FRIDAY
09.00	Prof. Jones (L) Macro-economics	Prof. Jones (S) Macro-economics	Mr Roberts (L) Micro-economics	Mr Roberts (L) Normative economics	Mr Roberts (S) Micro-economics
10.00	Mr Smith (L) Positive economics	Prof. Jones (T) Macro-economics	Mr Roberts (L) Inflation	Prof. Jones (S) Macro-economics	Mr Smith (T) Theories of Keynes
11.00	Mr Smith (L) Tools of economic analysis	Mr Smith (L) Theories of Keynes	Mr Smith (L) Inflation	Mr Roberts (S) Normative economics	Prof. Jones (T) Micro-economics
14.00			Mr Smith (S) Positive economics	Mr SMith (T) Positive economics	Mr Smith (T) Tools of economic analysis

L = lecture; S = seminar; T = tutorial

2. Now complete the conversation between two students below. Be careful which tense you use!

James: I (not see) _____ you at the party last night, Peter. Where (be) _____ you?

Peter: I (forget) _____ all about it. I (want) _____ to finish the essay over the weekend, so I (start) _____ on Friday afternoon and (keep) _____ going. But I (not finish) _____ it.

James: I (not finish) _____ the reading for that essay yet. I (go) _____ to the library yesterday, but none of the books I (need) _____ (be) _____ there.

Peter: I (never find) _____ all the books I want in that library since I (come) _____ to this college a year ago. Someone (just take) _____ them out each time I go there. Something ought to be done . . .

E. Understanding a lecture

You are now going to hear part of a lecture, divided into short sections to help you understand it. As you listen, answer the questions below.

Section 1——————————————————————————————
- The lecturer is going to examine three questions. Note down what they are.

_____

_____

_____

Section 2——————————————————————————————
- Is this statement correct or incorrect?
  Economists never get data directly from households.   ☐
- Note down two of the sources of data mentioned by the lecturer.

_____

_____

Section 3——————————————————————————————
- Note down the publication the lecturer refers to.

_____

- Complete the table with the figures the lecturer gives you.

TABLE 2-1 ████████████████████████████████

THE PRICE OF SILVER IN 1985
(US cents/troy ounce, New York, monthly averages)

JULY	AUGUST	SEPTEMBER	OCTOBER	NOVEMBER	DECEMBER

Source: IMF, *International Financial Statistics*

● Note down the term the lecturer explains to you.

_____

● Complete the figure according to the lecturer's instructions.

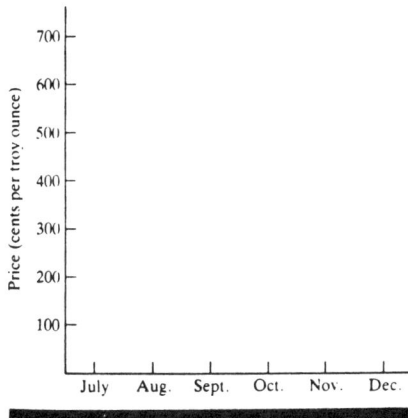

Section 5
Are these statements correct or incorrect?
● The lecturer says the table is easier to understand than the figure. ☐
● The high August price is more noticeable in the figure than the table. ☐
● The figure is less precise than the table. ☐

Section 6
● Note down the term the lecturer explains to you.

_____

● Note down what the term means.

_____

_____

_____

Section 7

TABLE 2-3

UNEMPLOYMENT BY AGE GROUP IN THE UK, 1985
(Thousands of workers unemployed)

	Under 18	18–19	20–24	25–34	35–44	45–54	55–59	60+
Unemployment	187	315	683	805	510	448	301	77

Source: Department of Employment _Gazette_.

Are these statements correct or incorrect?
● The lecturer gives an example of how to use the table. ☐
● Microeconomists are more likely to use this kind of data than macroeconomists. ☐
● Macroeconomists do not use time series data. ☐

2. Now wind the cassette back to the beginning of the lecture and listen to it again. This time, instead of answering questions, take notes. The questions you have already answered will help you do this. When you have listened to the whole of the lecture, you will be asked to give a short oral summary of it. So make sure you note down the important points of the lecture.

3. You should also write a summary of the lecture, based on your notes.

F. Understanding a printed text (2)

Read the following text carefully, looking up anything you do not understand.

2-2 INDEX NUMBERS

1 We often wish to compare numbers without emphasizing the units to which they refer. Suppose we want to know whether the price of silver has risen faster than the price of copper over the last 20 years. It may be more convenient to present the data as index numbers than to quote actual prices for specified quantities of silver or copper.

What an index number is

An *index number* expresses data relative to a given base value.

Table 2-4 shows annual averages for copper and silver prices in selected years. Looking at the top two rows, you will have to do some mental arithmetic to decide which price exhibited the larger percentage increase between 1960 and 1970. Suppose instead that we choose 1960 as the base year and assign the value 100 to the copper price index in this year. We assign the same value to the silver price index in this base year.

The procedure

2 Now consider 1970. The silver price of 177.1 cents per troy ounce is 1.9376 times the silver price in 1960. If we pretend that silver prices were 100 in 1960, this index must have risen to 193.76 by 1970. To calculate the 1985 value of the silver price index, we divide the 1985 silver price of 614.2 cents per troy ounce by the 1960 price of 91.40 cents per troy ounce to obtain 6.7199. Multiplying this by the starting value of 100 for the index in 1960, we obtain 617.99 as shown in Table 2-4. The price index for copper is calculated in the same way, dividing each price by the 1960 price and multiplying the answer by 100.

Check that you understand

3 Now check that you understand this procedure. In 1981 average silver prices were 1052.1 cents per troy ounce and average copper prices 83.99 cents per pound. What were the values of the silver and

▼

TABLE 2-4

PRICES OF SILVER AND COPPER
(silver in US cents/troy ounce, New York; copper in US cents/pound, US refining price; annual averages)

	1960	1970	1985
Silver (cents/troy ounce)	91.40	177.10	614.20
Copper (cents/pound)	32.05	57.67	65.57
Silver index (1960 = 100)	100	193.76	671.99
Copper index (1960 = 100)	100	179.94	204.59

Source: IMF, *International Financial Statistics*, 1985 Yearbook.

copper price indices? (Answer: 1151.09 and 262.06.) Looking at the last two rows of Table 2-4, it is now immediately apparent that between 1960 and 1985 the price of silver increased sixfold while the price of copper only doubled. The first two rows of the table contain the same information, but it cannot be interpreted so quickly.

4   Figure 2-3 plots price indices for average silver and copper prices for each year from 1964 to 1984, again using 1960 as the base year. The figure draws attention to the striking difference in behaviour between 1979 and 1981. You might not have noticed this in a table with numbers for each of these 22 years. Diagrams often draw attention to unusual behaviour of the variables that might pass unnoticed in a table.

Diagrams draw attention to unusual behaviour

Index Numbers as Averages

5 Suppose we now wish to know about movements in the price of metals as a whole. As we have seen, the prices of individual metals do not necesarily change in the same way. To derive a single measure

Average prices

FIGURE 2-3
INDICES OF THE PRICES OF SILVER AND COPPER, 1964–1984 (1960 = 100).
The two curves show price indices for silver and copper, using annual average data. The price of copper was rising over the period, with some periods of decline. The silver price reached an extraordinarily high level in 1980. The changes in the price of silver from 1979 to 1981 stand out very clearly in this figure. (*Source:* IMF, *International Financial Statistics*.)

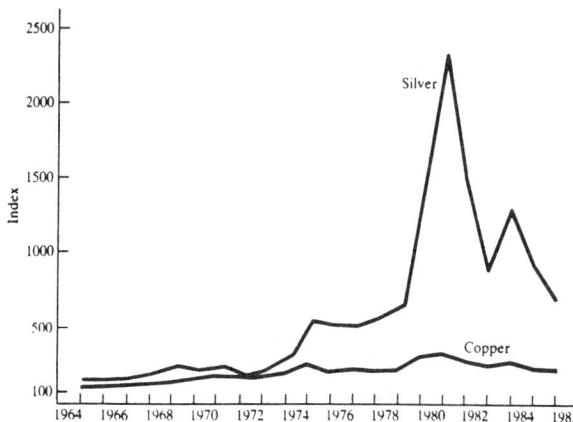

of metals prices we have to look at an *average* of different metal prices.

How to construct an index

6   Suppose copper and silver are the only two metals. To construct an index of all metal prices, we must make a single time series out of the two time series shown in the bottom two rows of Table 2-4. We give the price index of each metal a weight or share in the new index for metals as a whole. The weight should reflect the purpose for which the index is being constructed. If it is to be used to summarize what firms must pay for metal inputs, the weights should reflect the relative use of silver and copper as industrial inputs. Since copper is much more widely used than silver, we might decide to assign a weight of 0.8 to copper and 0.2 to silver. The weights are always chosen to add up to unity.

The weighted average

7   Table 2-5 shows how the metals price index, the *weighted average* of the indices for silver and copper, changes over time, In the base year 1960, the metals index is 100, being $(0.2 \times 100) + (0.8 \times 100)$. By 1970 the index has risen to 182.7, since this equals $(0.8 \times 179.94) + (0.2 \times 193.76)$. By 1985 the index stands at 298.07.

The metals index lies between the indices for the two separate metals

8   The metals index is a weighted average of silver and copper prices and must therefore lie between the indices for the two separate metals. The weights determine whether the metals index more closely resembles the behaviour of copper prices or the behaviour of silver prices. Because silver has a relatively low weight, the metals index does not rise nearly so sharply in 1980 as it would have done if a higher weight had been accorded to silver prices.

TABLE 2-5 ▬▬▬▬▬▬▬▬

PRICE INDICES FOR SILVER, COPPER, AND METALS
(1960 = 100, silver share = 0.2, copper share = 0.8)

	1960	1970	1985
Silver	100.0	193.76	671.99
Copper	100.0	179.94	204.59
Metals	100.0	182.7	298.07

Source: Calculated from Table 2-4.

G. Check your understanding

1. Look at the first paragraph again.
- Is this statement correct or incorrect?
  The writer says it is sometimes better to show data as index numbers rather than give
  the actual prices. ☐
- Can you explain the writer's definition of an index number in your own words?
- Is this statement correct or incorrect?
  The writer gives the value of 100 to silver in 1960. ☐

2. Look at paragraph 2 again. What words have the same meaning as:
- think about
- get
- work out mathematically

3. Look at paragraph 3 again.
- Can you explain in your own words why the answer is 1151.09 and 262.06?

4. Look at paragraph 4 again.
- Is this statement correct or incorrect?
  Tables show unusual behaviour better than diagrams. ☐

5. Look at paragraphs 5 and 6 again. What words have the same meaning as:
- get from
- make or build up
- give, put forward
- aim

6. Look at paragraph 7 again. How do you say the following?
- .   - +   - −
- ×   - ( )   - ÷

7. Look at paragraph 8 again. What words have the opposite meaning to:
- gradually
- for no reason
- looks unlike

H. Understanding discourse

Listen to a lecturer telling you the procedure to follow if you want to use the computer centre
on your own. Note down the procedure you must follow.

_____

_____

_____

_____

_____

1

T he following short test is for you to check whether you are learning the skills you will need to study Economics in English. It is for *your* information. It is *not* an examination. You may use a dictionary.

A. Reading

Read the following text and then answer the questions.

The Retail Price Index and Other Indices

What the RPI is

1 In the UK the most famous price index is the *retail price index* (RPI). Announced monthly, and closely watched by the news media and economic commentators, the RPI is an index of the prices of goods purchased by a typical household. It includes everything from food and housing to entertainment. The RPI is used to measure changes in the cost of living, the money that must be spent to purchase the typical bundle of goods consumed by a representative household. The percentage increase in the RPI over 12 months, comparing, say, its value in September 1987, with its value in September 1986, is the most widespread definition of the *inflation rate* in the UK.

How the RPI is constructed

2 The RPI is constructed in two stages. First, index numbers are calculated for each of the main categories of commodities purchased by households. For example, the index of food prices averages the price of individual foods such as coffee, bread, and milk. Again, the relative weights reflect the relative importance of the different commodities. Then the RPI is constructed by taking a weighted average of the different commodity groupings. Table 2-6 shows the weights used and the main commodity groupings. A 10 per cent rise in food prices will change the RPI more than a 10 per cent rise in tobacco prices because food has a much larger weight than tobacco.

Other indices

Other examples of indices are the index of wages in manufacturing, a weighted average of wages in different manufacturing industries, and the *Financial Times 30-share index*, a weighted average of the share prices of 30 of Britain's largest companies. Nor need the use of index numbers be confined to the *prices* of goods, labour, or

TABLE 2-6

WEIGHTS USED IN CONSTRUCTING THE RPI

ITEM	WEIGHT
Food	0.190
Transport and vehicles	0.156
Housing	0.153
Clothing and footwear	0.075
Alcohol	0.075
Miscellaneous goods	0.077
Services	0.062
Durable household goods	0.065
Fuel and light	0.065
Restaurant meals	0.045
Tobacco	0.037

Source: CSO, *Monthly Digest of Statistics.*

corporate shares. The *index of industrial production* is a weighted average of the *quantity* of goods produced by British industry. However, the procedure by which index numbers are calculated is always the same. We choose a base date and set the index equal to 100 at that date. Where the index refers to more than one commodity, we have to choose weights by which to average across the different commodities that the index describes.

Complete the following:

1. The RPI tells you how much:
   (a) industry pays for goods. ☐
   (b) people pay for goods used at home. ☐
   (c) money the government spends in a month. ☐
   (d) industry sells goods to the government for. ☐

2. Is this statement correct or incorrect?
   ● The RPI tells us how the cost of living has changed over a given period. ☐

3. The word *its* in paragraph 1, line 12, refers to
   (a) percentage increase. ☐
   (b) the RPI. ☐
   (c) 12 months. ☐
   (d) September, 1987. ☐

4. Is this statement correct or incorrect?
   ● The index number for food is calculated on the cost of one single food item. ☐

5. Is this statement correct or incorrect?
   ● The RPI does not take account of how important different commodities are. ☐

6. Is this statement correct or incorrect?
   ● Table 2-6 does not show all the items used in the RPI. ☐

▼

49

7. Is this statement correct or incorrect?
  - A 5 per cent rise in the cost of restaurant meals will not affect the RPI as much as a 5 per cent rise in the cost of clothes. ☐

8. Is this statement correct or incorrect?
  - Nobody has worked out an index to show how much people earn in manufacturing industry. ☐

9. Is this statement correct or incorrect?
  - Index numbers are worked out in different ways according to what is described in the index. ☐

10. Is this statement correct or incorrect?
  - Weights are only chosen if the index is set at 100. ☐

B. Writing

Study the following text and table. Then, using your own words, write a summary of the contents.

2-3 NOMINAL AND REAL VARIABLES

Table 2-7 shows data on wages and prices over the last decade. The top row shows an index of weekly wage rates of manual workers in British manufacturing industry. Weekly wage rates increased by more than four times between 1971 and 1983.

The index of weekly wage rates is constructed from data on weekly wage rates measured in pounds. We cannot say whether an increase in the value of this index made workers better off until we know what was happening to the prices of goods on which workers spend their incomes. The second row of Table 2-7 shows the behaviour of the RPI over the same period. Because of *inflation* – increases in the general price of goods – the four-fold increase in earnings between 1971 and 1983 certainly did not allow workers to purchase four times as many goods. For this reason we distinguish between nominal and real earnings.

Earnings measured in pounds, or indices based on such data, are said to be *nominal earnings. Real earnings* are calculated by adjusting nominal earnings for changes in the cost of living.

The third row of Table 2-7 calculates an index for real earnings of workers in all UK industries. Each number in the first row is divided by the

TABLE 2-7
NOMINAL AND REAL WAGE RATES IN MANUFACTURING
(1971 = 100 for all indices)

	1971	1973	1975	1977	1979	1981	1983
Index of weekly wage rates (manual workers)	100.0	128.3	195.3	245.1	333.1	427.0	476.7
Retail price index	100.0	117.0	168.6	227.6	279.6	384.3	419.4
Index of real weekly wage rates	100.0	109.7	115.6	107.8	119.0	111.2	114.0

Source: CSO, *Economic Trends.*

corresponding number in the second row then multiplied by 100. Real earnings measure the quantity of goods that could be purchased from the monthly wage income. From the third row of Table 2-7 we see that real earnings did rise between 1971 and 1983, but only by 14 per cent. Given the 319 per cent increase in goods prices, the 376 per cent increase in nominal earnings allowed wage-earners to increase by only 14 per cent the quantity of goods and services purchased out of wage income.

In fact, although nominal earnings rose steadily throughout the period, real earnings *fell* between 1975 and 1977. During these years nominal increases were large but were insufficient to offset even larger increases in the price of goods and services, so real earnings were reduced.

Only when inflation is zero will nominal and real indices move in the same way. This distinction between nominal and real values is widely used in economics and is especially important when the economy is experiencing high rates of inflation.

C. Listening

You will now hear part of a lecture. Listen to each section of the lecture twice. After you have listened to each section for the second time, answer the questions below.

Section 1
● What is the lecturer going to talk about?

● What currency is the lecturer going to use?

● Note down what this index measures.

TABLE 2-7
NOMINAL AND REAL WAGE RATES IN MANUFACTURING
(1971 = 100 for all indices)

	1971	1973	1975	1977	1979	1981	1983
Index of weekly wage rates (manual workers)	100.0	128.3	195.3	245.1	333.1	427.0	476.7
Retail price index	100.0	117.0	168.6	227.6	279.6	384.3	419.4
Index of real weekly wage rates	100.0	109.7	115.6	107.8	119.0	111.2	114.0

Source: CSO, *Economic Trends.*

Are these statements correct or incorrect?
- The term *nominal earnings* describes the money workers get paid each week. ☐
- *Real earnings* describes what workers can buy with the money they are paid. ☐

Section 3
- What happens to the purchasing power of the pound when the price of goods rises?

_____

- Note down what is used to measure nominal variables.

_____

- Note down what is used to measure real variables.

_____

Section 4
Are these statements correct or incorrect?
- 1971 pounds are used in the top row of Table 2-7. ☐
- Using 1971 pounds means that variables are being measured in real terms. ☐

A. Understanding a printed text (1)

The following text continues the topic of **the tools of economic analysis**. Look at the way it is divided into paragraphs. Pay attention to the heading and notes in the margin.

Now look at these questions:

1. Did everyone agree on the 'Fares Fair' policy?

2. What role does the writer ask you to take?
3. What is the purpose of equation (1)?
4. What does equation (2) represent?
5. What does the writer conclude about models?

Read the passage through and find the answers to those questions. Remember, you do not have to understand every word to answer them.

2-5 ECONOMIC MODELS

1 Now for an example of economics in action. In the early 1980s there was a controversy over the 'Fares Fair' policy of cutting bus and tube fares in London. Some people thought low fares would increase passengers and bring in extra revenue for London Transport, which runs the bus and tube services. Others thought that low fares would lead to disastrous losses in running London Transport. Eventually the matter was referred to the courts. Suppose you had been a consultant brought in to analyse the relationship between tube fares and revenue from running the tube: how would you have analysed the problem?

2　To organize our thinking, or – as economists describe it – to build a model, we require a simplified picture of reality which picks out the most important elements of the problem. We begin with the simple equation

Total fare collection
$$= \text{fare} \times \text{number of passengers} \quad (1)$$

In this stark form, equation (1) emphasizes, and thus organizes our thoughts around, two factors: the fare and the number of passengers. London Transport directly controls the fare, but can influence the number of passengers only through the fare that is set. (Cleaner stations and better service might also encourage passengers, but we neglect these effects for the moment.)

Pros and Cons of the 'Fares Fair' policy

The need to build a model

3 It might be argued that the number of passengers is determined by habit, convenience, and tradition, and is therefore completely unresponsive to changes in fares. This is *not* the view or model of traveller behaviour that an economist would initially adopt. It is possible to travel by car, bus, taxi, or tube, and decisions about the mode of transport are likely to be sensitive to the relative costs of the competing alternatives. Thus in equation (1) we must not view the number of passengers as fixed but develop a 'theory' or 'model' (we use these terms interchangeably) of what determines the number of passengers. We must model the *demand* for tube journeys.

4 In later chapters we study the theory of demand in detail. Applying a little common sense, we can probably work out the most important elements straight away. First, the fare itself matters. Other things equal, higher tube fares reduce the quantity of tube journeys demanded. Of course what matters is the price of the tube relative to the price of other means of tranport – cars, buses, and taxis. If their prices remain constant, lower tube fares will encourage tube passengers. Rises in the price of these other means of transport will also encourage tube passengers even though tube fares remain unaltered.

5 We now have a bare-bones model of the demand for tube journeys. We summarize this model in the formal statement:

**Quantity of tube journeys demanded
= *f*(tube fare, taxi fare, petrol price,
bus fare, . . .)** (2)

This statement reads as follows. The quantity of tube fares 'depends on', or 'is a function of', the tube fare, the taxi fare, petrol prices, bus fares, and some other things. The notation $f(\ \ )$ is just a shorthand for 'depends on all the things listed inside the brackets'. In equation (2) we have named explicitly the most important determinants of the demand for tube journeys. The row of dots reminds us that we have omitted some possible determinants of the demand for tube journeys in an effort to simplify our analysis. For example, tube demand probably depends on the temperature. It gets very uncomfortable in the underground when it is very hot. Since the purpose of our model is to study *changes* in the number of tube passengers, it will probably be all right to neglect the weather provided weather conditions are broadly the same every year.

6   To answer our original question, it is not sufficient to know the factors on which the demand for tube journeys depends. We need to know *how* the number of passengers varies with each of the factors we have identified in our model. Other things equal, we assume that an increase in tube fares will reduce tube passengers and that an increase in the price of any of the competing modes of transport will increase tube passengers. To make real progress, we shall somehow have to quantify each of these separate effects. Then, given predictions for bus and taxi fares and the price of petrol, we would be able to use our model to predict the number of tube passengers who would want to travel at each possible tube fare that might be set by London Transport. Multiplying the fare per journey by the predicted corresponding number of journeys demanded at this fare, we could then predict London Transport revenue given any decision about the level of tube fares.

To know the factors is not sufficient

7   Writing down a model is a safe way of forcing ourselves to look for all the relevant effects, to worry about which effects must be taken into account and which are minor and can probably be ignored in answering the question we have set ourselves. Without writing down a model, we might have forgotten about the influence of bus fares on tube journeys, an omission that might have led to serious errors in trying to understand and forecast revenue raised from tube fares.

The importance of a model

B. Check your understanding

Now read the text carefully, looking up any new items in a dictionary or reference book. Then answer the following questions:

1. What did some people think low fares would lead to?

2. What did others think the result would be?

3. Which two factors does equation (1) take account of?

4. Why does the economist not accept that the number of passengers is unresponsive to changes in fares?

▼

5. How are the most important elements of the model worked out?

6. What two factors will encourage tube passengers?

7. What does *f* mean in the equation?

8. What is the significance of . . . in the equation?

9. What else does the economist need to know, apart from the factors on which demand for tube journeys depends?

10. Summarise the process by which the writer says real progress can be made?

C. Increase your vocabulary

1. Look at the first paragraph again. What words have the same meaning as:
- income from taxes, fares etc.
- underground
- reducing in cost
- very bad, terrible
- result in
- imagine

2. Look at paragraph 2 again and explain the following words:
- model
- equation
- factors
- effects

3. Look at paragraph 3 again. What words have the opposite meaning to:
- at the end
- reject
- put off, discourage
- affected by

4. Look at paragraph 4 again. What words have the same meaning as:
- unchanged
- is of importance
- using
- immediately

5. Look at paragraph 5 again and explain the following words:
- bare-bones
- notation
- shorthand
- determinants

6. Look at paragraph 6 again. What words have the opposite meaning to:
- does not change
- unrelated
- not shown

7. Look at paragraph 7 again. What words have the opposite meaning to:
- inclusion
- unimportant, not mattering
- major

8. These words have occurred in the text. Using your dictionary, complete the following table:

Noun	Verb	Adjective
	analyse	
		simple
	argue	
theory		
quantity		
	compete	
progress		

D. Check your grammar

1. ASKING QUESTIONS

Can you ask questions in a way that makes sure that you get the information you want? And that you understand the answers? Look at the table below. It is blank. When it is complete, it will give you some information on fares and passenger kilometres on the London Underground from 1973 to 1983. The teacher has the information you need to complete the table. Ask the questions you need and complete the table. Start by asking about the headings.

Table 2-8
Fares and Passenger Kilometres on the London Underground, 1973–83

Year

Sources:

You now have to write a short explanation of the table you have completed. The teacher has the information you need to do this. Ask for the information you need and note down the answers. Then write a short explanation.

_____

_____

_____

_____

_____

_____

_____

_____

E. Understanding a lecture

You are now going to hear part of a lecture, divided into short sections to help you understand it. As you listen, answer the questions below.

FIGURE 2-4

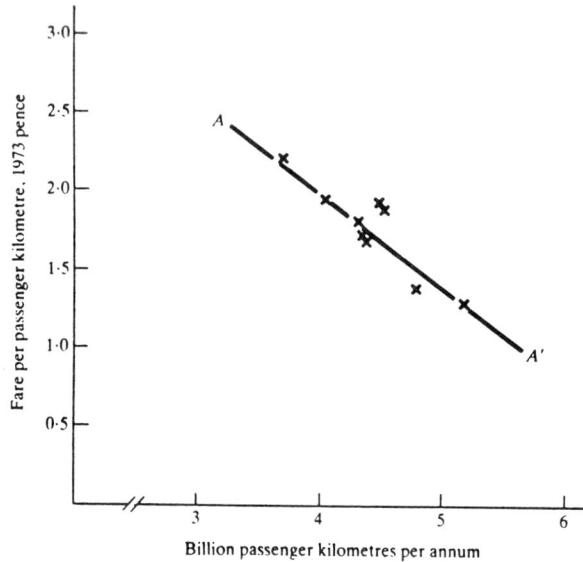

Billion passenger kilometres per annum

Section 1
● What kind of diagram is the lecturer talking about?

_____

- Is this statement correct or incorrect?
  The diagram gives the same information as Table 2-8. ☐

Section 2————————————————————————
- Note down what this kind of diagram shows.

  _____

- Is this statement correct or incorrect?
  The vertical column shows the same information as column 2 in the table. ☐

Section 3————————————————————————
- Note down which column in the table is measured along the horizontal axis.

  _____

- Which columns in the table are plotted in the diagram?

  _____

Section 4————————————————————————
- Put the cross where the lecturer tells you to in the diagram.

Section 5————————————————————————
- Note down what each cross shows.

  _____

Section 6————————————————————————
- Is this statement correct or incorrect?
  The lecturer thinks the table is easier to understand than the diagram. ☐
- Note down what the diagram suggests on average.

  _____

Section 7————————————————————————
- Note down what the line A A' might describe.

  _____

- Is this statement correct or incorrect?
  When real bus and taxi fares are high, the crosses will lie to the left of the line. ☐

Section 8————————————————————————
- Is this statement correct or incorrect?
  The factor that the crosses are close to the line shows that tube fares do affect passenger use. ☐

2. Now wind the cassette back to the beginning of the lecture and listen to it again. This time, instead of answering questions, take notes. The questions you have already answered will help you do this. When you have listened to the whole of the lecture, you will be asked to give a short oral summary of it. So make sure you note down the important points of the lecture.

3. You should also write a summary of the lecture, based on your notes.

F. Understanding a printed text (2)

The following text continues the topic of **scatter diagrams**. Read it carefully looking up anything you do not understand.

How Table 2-9 is calculated

> ## Scatter Diagrams
>
> 1   Table 2-9 examines the relation between the real tube fare and real revenue that London **Transport** obtains from selling tube tickets. Real revenue is simply the real fare per passenger kilometre multiplied by the number of passenger kilometres travelled. The first column of Table 2-9 is obtained by multiplying together data in the last two columns of Table 2-8. For example, for 1973 we multiply 1.50 pence per passenger kilometre by 5225 million passenger kilometres to obtain £78.4 million revenue. For 1974 we multiply 1.29 pence per passenger kilometre by 5166 million passenger kilometres to obtain £66.6 million revenue. This is a figure for *real* revenue, since it is measured at 1973 prices which already correct for inflation between 1973 and 1974. It is measured at 1973 prices because we calculated the figure from the price of 1.29 pence per passenger kilometre, which itself had already been expressed in 1973 prices. Column (2) simply reproduces column (3) of Table 2-8.

TABLE 2-8

FARES AND PASSENGER KILOMETRES ON THE LONDON UNDERGROUND, 1973–83

YEAR	(1) FARE PER PASSENGER KILOMETRE (pence)	(2) RPI (1973 = 100)	(3) REAL FARE PER PASSENGER KILOMETRE (1973 pence)	(4) PASSENGER KILOMETRES (millions)
1973	1.50	100.0	1.50	5224
1974	1.50	116.0	1.29	5166
1975	1.98	144.1	1.37	4775
1976	2.80	167.9	1.67	4355
1977	3.33	194.5	1.71	4344
1978	3.93	210.7	1.87	4506
1979	4.58	238.9	1.92	4464
1980	5.97	281.8	2.12	4253
1081	6.14	315.4	1.95	4091
1982	7.55	342.5	2.20	3661
1983	6.44	358.2	1.80	4300

Sources: Department of Transport, *Transport Statistics Great Britain 1973–83*; CSO, *Economic Trends.*

TABLE 2-9

REAL TUBE FARES AND REAL REVENUE, 1973-83

YEAR	(1) REAL REVENUE (£ million, at 1973 prices)	(2) REAL TUBE FARES PER PASSENGER KILOMETRE (pence, at 1973 prices)
1973	78.4	1.50
1974	66.6	1.29
1975	65.4	1.37
1976	72.7	1.67
1977	74.2	1.71
1978	84.3	1.87
1979	85.7	1.92
1980	90.2	2.12
1981	79.8	1.95
1982	80.5	2.20
1983	77.4	1.80

Source: taken from Table 2-8.

2   The years of highest real revenue coincide with the years in which the real tube fare was highest. To the extent that we are prepared to neglect the other factors identified in our model of passenger use and pretend that changes in real fares were the only cause of changes in use, Table 2-9 offers a clear answer to our original question. Raising real tube fares reduces passenger use, but not sufficiently to compensate for the fact that fares are higher. Revenue, being fares times passenger use, rises in real terms when real fares are increased.

Table 2-9 answers our question

3   Figure 2-5 plots the data of Table 2-9 in a scatter diagram. As in Figure 2-4, we could draw a line through these crosses to capture the average relation between fares and revenue in the 1970s. Such a line would slope up, indicating that higher fares were associated with higher revenue.

The same data presented in a scatter diagram

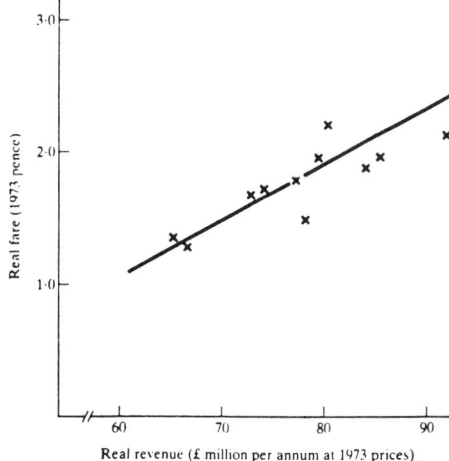

FIGURE 2-5 SCATTER DIAGRAM OF REAL TUBE FARES AND REAL REVENUES. This diagram shows the relation between real tube fares and real revenue over the period 1973-83. Higher fares are associated with higher revenue.

4 How confident can we be that we have found the right answer to our question? However suggestive the diagrams, all we have really discovered is that fares went up and passenger use did not fall sufficiently to make total revenue go down. Only if other determinants of passenger usage remained constant can we infer that higher fares cause higher revenue. Perhaps higher real petrol prices and higher parking charges made tube revenue rise *in spite of* higher prices. Perhaps lower prices would have captured so many commuters who abandoned their cars in favour of buses that revenue might have risen even more. Until we investigate whether or not other determinants of passenger demand changed over the 1970s, our analysis so far is suggestive but not conclusive. We return to this question shortly.

Our analysis is suggestive, not conclusive

G. Check your understanding

1. Look at the first paragraph again and answer these questions.
● What relationship is shown in Table 2-9?
● In Table 2-9 real revenue for 1975 is shown as 65.4. How is this figure calculated?
● In column 2 of Table 2-9, the fare for 1983 is shown as 1.80. Does this figure take account of inflation?
2. Look at paragraph 2 again and answer this question.
● The writer says Table 2-9 'offers a clear answer to our original question'. Explain in your own words what this answer is.
3. Look at paragraph 3 again and answer this question.
● What does the line in the scatter diagram show?
4. Look at paragraph 4 again and answer this question.
● The writer concludes that the analysis is 'suggestive' not 'conclusive'. Can you explain why he says this?

H. Understanding discourse

Listen to a lecturer giving a reading list to some students. As you listen, write down what the students are to read.

_____

_____

_____

_____

_____

_____

SUPPLY & DEMAND (1)

A. Understanding a printed text (1)

The following text will introduce you to the topic of **supply and demand**. Look at the way it is divided into sections and paragraphs. Pay attention to the headings in the margin and to the table.

Now look at these questions:

1. Do different markets carry out different economics functions?
2. In the first section the writer refers to three questions he has talked about before. What are they?
3. Can you explain what the writer means by *demand*?
4. Can you explain what the writer means by *supply*?
5. Does the writer explain what he means by *equilibrium*?

Read the passage through and find the answers to those questions. Remember, you do not have to understand every word to answer them.

3-1 THE MARKET

1   In Chapter 1 we defined markets in a very general way as arrangements through which prices guide resource allocation. We now adopt a narrower definition.

> A *market* is a set of arrangements by which buyers and sellers are in contact to exchange goods or services.

A narrower definition of a market

Some markets (shops and fruit stalls) physically bring together the buyer and the seller. Other markets (the London Stock Exchange) operate chiefly through intermediaries (stockbrokers) who transact business on behalf of clients. In supermarkets, sellers choose the price, stock the shelves, and leave customers to choose whether or not to make a purchase. Antique auctions force buyers to bid against each other with the seller taking a passive role.

Different kinds of market

2   Although superficially different, these markets perform the same economic function. They determine prices that ensure that the quantity people wish to buy equals the quantity people wish to sell. Price and quantity cannot be considered separately. In establishing that the price of a Rolls Royce is ten times the price of a small Ford, the market for motor cars simultaneously ensures that production and sales of small Fords will greatly exceed the production and sales of Rolls Royces. These prices guide society in choosing what, how, and for whom to purchase.

These markets carry out the same functions

3   To understand this process more fully, we require a model of a typical market. The essential features on which such a model must concentrate are demand, the behaviour of buyers, and supply, the behaviour of sellers. It will then be possible to study the interaction of these forces to see how a market works in practice.

We need a model to understand the process

▼

3-2 DEMAND, SUPPLY, AND EQUILIBRIUM

What demand is

Demand is not a particular quantity

What supply is

Supply is not a particular quantity

4   *Demand* is the quantity of a good buyers wish to purchase at each conceivable price.

Thus demand is not a particular quantity, such as six bars of chocolate, but rather a full description of the quantity of chocolate the buyer would purchase at each and every price which might be charged. The first column of Table 3-1 shows a range of prices for bars of chocolate. The second column shows the quantities that might be demanded at these prices. Even when chocolate is free, only a finite amount will be wanted. People get sick from eating too much chocolate. As the price of chocolate rises, the quantity demanded falls, other things equal. We have assumed that nobody will buy any chocolate when the price is more than £0.40 per bar. Taken together, columns (1) and (2) describe the demand for chocolate as a function of its price.

    Supply is the quantity of a good sellers wish to sell at each conceivable price.

Again, supply is not a particular quantity but a complete description of the quantity that sellers would like to sell at each and every possible price. The third column of Table 3-1 shows how much chocolate sellers wish to sell at each price. Chocolate cannot be produced for nothing. Nobody would wish to supply if they receive a zero price. In our example, it takes a price of at least £0.20 per bar before there is any incentive to

TABLE 3-1

THE DEMAND FOR AND SUPPLY OF CHOCOLATE

(1) PRICE (£/bar)	(2) DEMAND (million bars/year)	(3) SUPPLY (million bars/year)
0.00	200	0
0.10	160	0
0.20	120	40
0.30	80	80
0.40	40	120
0.50	0	160
0.60	0	200
0.70	0	240

supply chocolate. At higher prices it becomes increasingly lucrative to supply chocolate bars and there is a corresponding increase in the quantity of bars that would be supplied. Taken together, columns (1) and (3) describe the supply of chocolate bars as a function of their price.

5   Notice the distinction between *demand* and the *quantity demanded*. Demand describes the behaviour of buyers at every price. At a particular price such as £0.30, there is a particular quantity demanded, namely 80 million bars/year. The term 'quantity demanded' makes sense only in relation to a particular price. A similar distinction applies to *supply* and *quantity supplied*.

6   In everyday language, we would say that when the demand for football tickets exceeds their supply some people will not get into the ground. Economists must be more precise. At the price charged for tickets, the quantity demanded exceeded the quantity supplied. Although the size of the ground sets an upper limit on the quantity of tickets that can be supplied, a higher ticket price would have reduced the quantity demanded, perhaps leaving empty space in the ground. Yet there has been no change in demand, the schedule describing how many people want admission at each possible ticket price. The quantity demanded has changed because the price has changed.

7   As in our discussion of tube fares in the previous chapter, we must recognize that the demand schedule relating price and quantity demanded and the supply schedule relating price and quantity supplied are each constructed on the assumption of 'other things equal'. In the demand for tube tickets, the 'other things' were the cost of alternative modes of transport. In the demand for football tickets, one of the 'other things' that is important is whether or not the game is being shown on television. If it is, the quantity of tickets demanded at each and every price will be lower than if the game is not televised. To understand how a market works, we must first explain why demand and supply are what they are. (Is the game on television? Has the ground capacity been extended by building a new stand?) Then we must examine how the price adjusts to balance the

The distinction between demand and quantity demanded

The assumption of 'other things equal'

The effect of 'other things'

quantities supplied and demanded, given the underlying supply and demand schedules relating quantity to price.

8   Let us think again about the market for chocolate described in Table 3-1. Other things equal, *the lower the price of chocolate, the higher the quantity demanded.* Other things equal, *the higher the price of chocolate, the higher the quantity supplied.* A campaign by dentists warning of the effect of chocolate on tooth decay, or a fall in household incomes, would change the 'other things' relevant to the demand for chocolate. Either of these changes would reduce the demand for chocolate, reducing the quantities demanded at each price. Cheaper cocoa beans, or technical advances in packaging chocolate bars, would change the 'other things' relevant to the supply of chocolate bars. They would tend to increase the supply of chocolate bars, increasing the quantity supplied at each possible price.

B. Check your understanding

Now read the text carefully, looking up any new items in a dictionary or reference book. Then answer the following questions:

1. What difference does the writer point to between a fruit stall and the London Stock Exchange?

2. What makes sure that the quantity people want to buy is the same as the quantity people want to sell?

3. What influence do prices have on society?

4. What is the demand for chocolate?

5. What happens when the price of chocolate rises?

6. What is the supply of chocolate?

7. What do columns 1 and 3 of Table 3-1 describe?

8. In the writer's example, why has the quantity of football tickets that people want changed?

9. Can you explain what the writer means by 'other things equal'?

10. What 'other things' would reduce the demand for chocolate?

▼

C. Increase your vocabulary

1. Look at the first paragraph again. Can you explain the following words:
- stall
- intermediaries
- stockbrokers
- supermarkets
- auctions

2. Look at paragraph 2 again. What words have the same meaning as:
- at the same time
- apart
- on the surface
- be greater than

3. Look at paragraph 3 again. What words have the opposite meaning to:
- in theory
- unimportant
- pay no attention to

4. Look at paragraph 4 again. Complete the following sentences, using words from the paragraph.
- Would you believe it? That shop _____ me 40p for a bar of chocolate!
- As there are only so many people in the country, the number of cars required is _____.

- Although I could not prove it, I _____ the figures in the table were correct.
- If people cannot sell a particular good, there is no _____ to produce it.
- My friend wants to make a lot of money, so he's looking for a _____ business to take over.

5. Look at paragraphs 5 and 6 again. What words have the opposite meaning to:
- expulsion
- inexact
- is nonsense
- lower

6. Look at paragraph 7 again. Write a sentence showing you understand the meaning of the words:
- schedule
- alternative
- adjust
- balance

7. Look at paragraph 8 again. What words have the opposite meaning to:
- retreats
- bearing no relation to

D. Check your grammar

1. CHECKING NOTES

> **Do you remember?**
> *Instead of saying* that, he *should have said* . . .

Now look at the following notes a student has made on the text. Say if the notes are accurate or not. If they are not, give the correct version.

- Auctions operate through intermediaries.
- Different markets perform different economic functions.
- Demand is the behaviour of sellers.
- Supply is the behaviour of buyers
- Supply is a particular quantity of a good.
- Cols 1 & 3, Table 3-1, show the supply of chocolate bars as a function of their price.
- Demand means the behaviour of sellers at one fixed price.
- Supply and quantity supplied mean the same.

Make complete sentences out of the following notes, putting the verbs in brackets in the right tense. Then arrange the sentences into a paragraph. Make sure that the sentences follow each other logically and that the paragraph makes sense.

- computers/relationships/econometricians/simultaneously/average/many/to fit/between/ variables (use)

- diagrams/relationships/between/the/two/plotted/variables/in/scatter/diagram/the (show)

- to get round/us/other-things-equal/this/the/problem/in principle/dimensions/always/two/ in/which (allow; apply)

- possible/through/it/to fit/the/a/points/line/these/relationship/between/average/ to summarise/variables/two/the (be)

E. Understanding a lecture

You will now hear part of a lecture, divided into short sections to help you understand it. As you listen, answer the questions below.

Section 1
- What have the students already read about?

- Note down what the lecture will be about.

Section 2

TABLE 3-1

THE DEMAND FOR AND SUPPLY OF CHOCOLATE

(1) PRICE (£/bar)	(2) DEMAND (million bars/year)	(3) SUPPLY (million bars/year)
0.00	200	0
0.10	160	0
0.20	120	40
0.30	80	80
0.40	40	120
0.50	0	160
0.60	0	200
0.70	0	240

Are these statements correct or incorrect?
- The lecturer's intention is to model how the market works. ☐
- At low prices supply exceeds demand. ☐
- At high prices supply exceeds demand. ☐

Section 3

- What word does the lecturer use to mean 'in the middle'?

_____

- What term does the lecturer use to describe the price at which demand equals supply?

_____

Section 4

- In this example, how does the lecturer describe 80 million bars?

_____

- Note down what the lecturer means by 'excess demand'.

_____

Section 5

- Note down the term the lecturer tells you to.

_____

- Note down what the term means.

_____

Section 6

Are these statements correct or incorrect?
- If sellers cannot sell their chocolate they will reduce their prices. ☐
- Price-cutting does not reduce the number of bars producers want to sell. ☐

Section 7

Are these statements correct or incorrect?
- Sellers will not increase prices if they run out of stock. ☐
- Prices will rise until the equilibrium price is reached. ☐

2. Now wind the cassette back to the beginning of the lecture and listen to it again. This time, instead of answering questions, take notes. The questions you have already answered will help you do this. When you have listened to the whole of the lecture, you will be asked to give a short oral summary of it. So make sure you note down the important points of the lecture.

3. You should also write a summary of the lecture, based on your notes.

▼

F. Understanding a printed text (2)

Read the following text carefully, looking up anything you do not understand.

3-3 DEMAND AND SUPPLY CURVES

1 Table 3-1 shows demand and supply conditions in the chocolate market and allows us to find the equilibrium price and quantity. It is convenient to approach the same problem diagrammatically using demand and supply curves.

What the demand curve shows

2 The *demand curve* shows the relation between price and quantity demanded, holding other things constant. In Figure 3-1 we measure on the vertical axis prices of chocolate bars. Corresponding quantities demanded in millions of bars per year are measured on the horizontal axis. The demand curve plots the data in the first two columns of Table 3-1. The point A shows that 160 million bars per year are demanded at a price of £0.10. The point B shows that 120 million bars per year are demanded at a price of £0.20. Plotting all the

FIGURE 3-1 THE DEMAND CURVE FOR CHOCOLATE BARS.   The demand curve shows the negative relation between price and quantity demanded, holding other things equal. The vertical axis measures the price of chocolate bars and the horizontal axis measures the quantity demanded. The diagram plots the points in the first two columns of Table 3-1. Point A shows that 160 million bars per year are demanded at £0.10. Point B shows that 120 million bars per year are demanded at £0.20. Plotting all the points and joining them up, we obtain the demand curve.

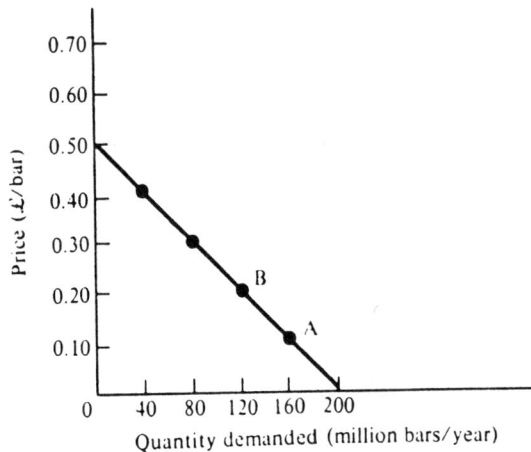

points and joining them up, we obtain the demand curve. In our example, this curve happens to be a straight line. As expected, it has a negative slope showing that larger quantities are demanded at lower prices.

3   The *supply curve* shows the relation between price and quantity supplied, holding other things constant. In Figure 3-2 we plot the supply information given by columns (1) and (3) of Table 3-1. Again we join up the different data points.

4   In Figure 3-3 we show the demand curve, labelled *DD*, and the supply curve, labelled *SS*, in the same diagram. We can now re-examine our analysis of excess supply, excess demand, and

What the supply curve shows

The demand and supply curves together

FIGURE 3-2 THE SUPPLY CURVE FOR CHOCOLATE BARS. The supply curve shows the positive relation between the price and quantity supplied, holding other things equal. The diagram plots the points in the first and third columns of Table 3-1. Again we join up the points.

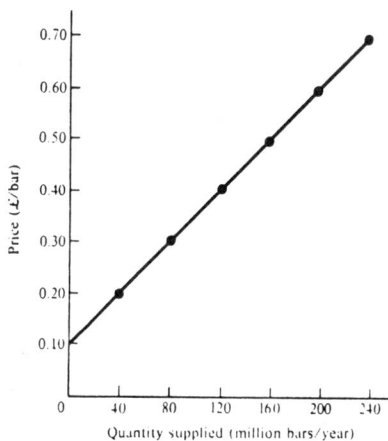

FIGURE 3-3 THE MARKET FOR CHOCOLATE BARS. Market equilibrium occurs at the point *E*, where the price is £0.30; there, the quantity demanded equals quantity supplied equals 80 million bars per year. At prices below the equilibrium price there is excess demand: *AB* shows the excess demand at the price £0.20. At prices above the equilibrium price there is excess supply: *FG* shows the excess supply at the price £0.40.

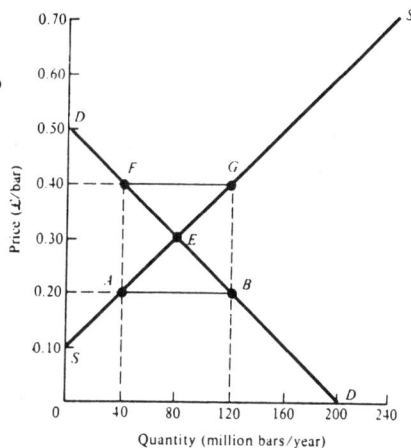

equilibrium. Consider a particular price as represented by a height on the vertical axis. At a price below the equilibrium price, the horizontal distance between the supply curve and the demand curve at this height shows the excess demand at this price. For example, at £0.20 the quantity supplied is 40 million bars per year, the quantity demanded 120 million bars per year, and the distance AB represents the excess demand of 80 million bars per year. Conversely, at a price above the equilibrium price there is excess supply. At £0.40, 40 million bars per year are demanded, 120 million bars per year are supplied and the horizontal distance FG measures the excess supply of 80 million bars per year at this price.

5   Suppose the price is £0.40. Only 40 million bars per year are sold even though sellers would like to sell 120 million bars per year. How do we know that it is sellers not buyers who are frustrated when their wishes differ? Participation in a market is voluntary. Buyers are not *forced* to buy nor sellers forced to sell. When markets are not in equilibrium, the quantity transacted must be the *smaller* of the quantity supplied and the quantity demanded. Any quantity larger than 40 million bars per year at a price of £0.40 would involve buyers in forced purchases. Similarly, when the price is £0.20, any quantity larger than 40 million bars per year would involve sellers in forced sales.

6   Market equilibrium is shown by the intersection of the demand curve DD and the supply curve SS, at a price of £0.30, at which 80 million bars per year are transacted. At any other price, the quantity traded is the smaller of the quantity demanded and the quantity supplied. We can now reconsider *price determination* in the chocolate market. Figure 3-3 implies that there is excess supply at all prices above the equilibrium price of £0.30. Sellers react to unsold stocks by cutting prices. Only when prices have been reduced to the equilibrium price will excess supply be eliminated. The equilibrium position is shown by the point E. Conversely, at prices below £0.30 there is excess demand, which bids up the price of chocolate, gradually eliminating excess demand until the equilibrium point E is reached. In equilibrium buyers and sellers can trade as much as they wish at the equilibrium price and there is no incentive for any further price changes.

Market equilibrium is where the curves DD and SS intersect

Price determination reconsidered

G. Check your understanding

Now look at the following questions. Refer back to the text and make notes to enable you to answer the following:

● Can you explain what a demand curve is?

_____

_____

● Can you explain how Figure 3-1 is constructed?

_____

_____

● Can you explain what a supply curve is?

_____

_____

● Can you explain how Figure 3-2 is constructed?

_____

_____

● Can you explain what Figure 3-3 shows?

_____

_____

● The writer reconsiders 'price determination'. What points does he make?

_____

_____

H. Understanding discourse

A tutor is giving some students some advice. Listen to what he says and note down what you should do if you follow his advice.

_____

_____

_____

_____

SUPPLY & DEMAND (2)

A. Understanding a printed text (1)

The following text continues the topic of **demand, supply and the market**. Look at the way it is divided into sections and paragraphs. Pay attention to the headings and notes in the margin.

Now look at these questions:

1. From the heading, what do you expect this text to be about?
2. What do you think the writer's purpose is in paragraphs 2 to 4?
3. What do you think the writer's purpose is in paragraph 5?
4. Can you explain in your own words what the difference between a normal and an inferior good is?
5. What do you think the writer's purpose in paragraph 6 is?

Read the passage through and find the answers to those questions. Remember, you do not have to understand every word to answer them.

3-4 BEHIND THE DEMAND CURVE

1 The demand curve in Figures 3-1 and 3-3, like the data in column (2) of Table 3-1, depicts the relation between price and quantity demanded *holding other things constant*. What are those 'other things'? The other things relevant to demand curves can usually be grouped under three headings: the price of related goods, the income of consumers (buyers), and consumer tastes or preferences. We look at each of these in turn.

What are those 'other things'?

The Price of Related Goods

2 In Chapter 2 we discussed the demand for tube travel. We saw that a rise in bus fares or petrol prices would increase the quantity of tube travel demanded at each possible price. In everyday language, we think of buses and private cars as *substitutes* for the tube. Loosely speaking, this means that a journey may be made by bus or car instead of by tube. More precisely, an increase in the price of buses or cars will lead to an increase in the demand for tube travel. Economists use an even more precise definition of substitutes which we shall encounter in Chapter 5, but everyday language gives the right idea of what we mean. Similarly, everyday language suggests that petrol and cars are *complements* because you cannot use a car without also using petrol. A rise in the price of petrol tends to reduce the demand for cars. Again, everyday language gives the right idea although an exact definition of complements will not be given until Chapter 5.

Buses and cars are substitutes

Petrol and cars are complements

3   How do these ideas about substitutes and complements relate to the demand for chocolate bars? Clearly, other sweets (mint drops and jelly babies) are substitutes for chocolate. We expect an increase in the price of other sweets to increase the quantity of chocolate demanded at each possible chocolate price, as people substitute away from other sweets towards chocolate. If people buy chocolate to eat at the cinema, films would be a complement for bars of chocolate. A rise in the price of cinema tickets would reduce the demand for chocolate since fewer people will go to the cinema. Nevertheless, it is difficult to think of a lot of goods that are complements for chocolate. This suggests, correctly, that most of the time goods are substitutes for each other. Complementarity, while present in many instances, is usually a more specific feature (record players and records, coffee and milk, shoes and shoelaces).

Complements and substitutes related to chocolate bars

4   Before we leave the influence of prices of related goods on the demand for a particular commodity, it should be noted that the development of new products can be viewed within this framework. Technological advances that make possible hand calculators, low fuel consumption cars, or low-calorie beer affect the demand for related goods. One way to think about this is to say that the new product had always been available, but previously its price had been prohibitively high so that nobody could afford it. The technological advance enables the new product to be made available at a much lower price. This will stimulate demand for goods that are complements to the new product (video games may increase the demand for televisions on which they can be played in the home) but reduce the demand for substitutes for the new product (being able to watch films on a home video reduces the demand for going to the cinema).

New products can be viewed within this framework

Consumer Incomes

5 The second category of 'other things equal' when we draw a particular demand curve is consumer income. When incomes rise, the demand for most goods increases. Typically, consumers buy more of everything. However, there are exceptions.

A *normal good* is a good for which demand increases when incomes rise. An *inferior good* is a good for which demand falls when incomes rise.

As their name suggests, most goods are normal goods. An example of an inferior good might be cheap but nasty cuts of meat. As household incomes rise, households spend absolutely less on cheap cuts and more on better cuts of meat such as steaks. Inferior goods are typically cheap but low-quality goods which people would prefer not to buy if they could afford to spend a little more.

Tastes

6 The third category of things held constant along a particular demand curve is consumer tastes or preferences. In part, these are shaped by convenience, custom, and social attitudes. When the Beatles and the Rolling Stones first became popular, the demand for haircuts suddenly fell. The fashion for the mini-skirt reduced the demand for textile material. More recently, the emphasis on health and fitness has increased the demand for jogging equipment, health foods, and sports facilities while reducing the demand for cream cakes, butter, and cigarettes.

B. Check your understanding

Now read the text carefully, looking up any new items in a dictionary or reference book. Then answer the following questions:

1. What three things are relevant to demand curves?

2. Why are buses and cars substitutes for the tube?

3. Why is petrol a complement to a car?

4. Are the definitions of substitutes and complements that the writer gives here precise?

5. What are substitutes for chocolate?

6. What are most goods substitutes for?

7. Does the writer's framework apply to new products?

8. Can you think of an example of a normal good?

9. Can you think of an example of an inferior good?

10. Why has the demand for cigarettes fallen recently?

C. Increase your vocabulary

1. Look at the first paragraph again. What words have the same meaning as:
- unchanging
- shows
- one after the other

2. Look at paragraph 2 again. What words have the opposite meaning to:
- precisely
- not usually used
- public

3. Look at paragraph 3 again. Complete the following sentences using words from the paragraph.
- Ink could be described as a _____ to a pen.
- If paper gets more expensive there's bound to be an _____ in the price of books.

- I _____ the government will increase taxes next year.
- I suppose you could say a pipe is a _____ for cigarettes.
- My tutor gave me some _____ advice on how to improve my written work.

4. Look at paragraph 4 again. What words correspond to these definitions:
- tending to prevent the purchase of something
- useful article of trade
- excite, rouse

5. Look at paragraphs 5 and 6 again. Can you explain the following:
- category
- consumer income
- exceptions
- custom
- social attitudes

Do you remember?
Some words belong naturally together. These are called collocations; for example:
a simple misunderstanding . . . we approach the problem . . .

---

6. Choose the word that collocates best with the word in *italics*. Remember, the other words may not be 'wrong', just not as natural.
- In times of inflation we all suffer from rising   *prices*. ☐
  - ascending ☐
  - climbing ☐
- All markets act   the same *function*. ☐
  - perform ☐
  - do ☐
- I want to work out an entire   *description* of the demand for chocolate. ☐
  - a whole ☐
  - a complete ☐
- At £0.20 the *quantity* given   is 40 million bars. ☐
  - provided ☐
  - supplied ☐
- Factories must obey certain *safety* needs. ☐
  - demands. ☐
  - requirements. ☐
- This table brings up   several *questions*. ☐
  - asks ☐
  - raises ☐
- The table shows wages in the manufacturing *industries*. ☐
  - producing ☐
  - making ☐
- People spend more in a time of descending *prices*. ☐
  - falling ☐
  - slipping ☐

D. Check your grammar

Complete the following paragraph, using *(al)though* or *whereas*

_____ Anne works extremely hard, she finds her Economics option very hard work. She spends a great deal of time on it, _____ she never gets good marks, _____ her friend Karen gets high marks with hardly any effort at all. _____ Karen helps Anne as much as she can, it doesn't seem to make any difference. So _____ Karen is quite happy with her course, Anne is thinking of changing subjects at the end of term, _____ that will be difficult.

E. Understanding a lecture

You are now going to hear part of a lecture, divided into short sections to help you understand it. As you listen, answer the questions below.

Section 1
- What is the lecturer going to talk about?

_____

- Note down the three factors that will change the demand for chocolate

_____

Section 2
Are these statements correct or incorrect?
- The lecturer says ice cream is a complement to chocolate. ☐
- When ice cream prices are high the demand for chocolate rises. ☐

Section 3

TABLE 3-2
THE EFFECT OF AN INCREASE IN THE PRICE OF ICE CREAM ON THE DEMAND FOR CHOCOLATE

PRICE OF CHOCOLATE (£/bar)	DEMAND FOR CHOCOLATE AT LOW ICE CREAM PRICE (million bars/year)	DEMAND FOR CHOCOLATE AT HIGH ICE CREAM PRICE (million bars/year)
0.00	200	280
0.10	160	240
0.20	120	200
0.30	80	160
0.40	40	120
0.50	0	80
0.60	0	40
0.70	0	0

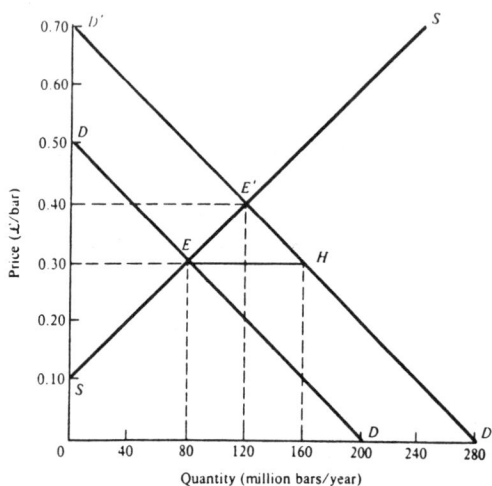

- Note down the letters which show the new demand curve.

_____

- Is this statement correct or incorrect?
  The demand curve has shifted to the right because people want more chocolate. ☐

78

Section 4
● Note down the letter which shows the new equilibrium price.

_____

Section 5
● Note down how excess demand is shown in the figure.

_____

● Is this statement correct or incorrect?
  At a price of 30p 80 million bars are demanded.   ☐

Section 6
● Is this statement correct or incorrect?
  A higher price has no effect on the quantity demanded.   ☐

Section 7
● Note down the additional factor the lecturer points to.

_____

● Is this statement correct or incorrect?
  Economists sometimes do not show price when drawing demand curves.   ☐

2. Now wind the cassette back to the beginning of the lecture and listen to it again. This time, instead of answering questions, take notes. The questions you have already answered will help you do this. When you have listened to the whole of the lecture, you will be asked to give a short oral summary of it. So make sure you note down the important points.

3. You should also write a summary of the lecture, based on your notes.

F. Understanding a printed text (2)

Read the following text carefully, looking up anything you do not understand.

3-6 BEHIND THE SUPPLY CURVE

1 Before discussing changes that shift supply curves, we discuss in greater detail why increases in price increase the quantity supplied, holding constant all other factors. At low prices, only the most efficient chocolate producers will be able to make any profits producing chocolate. As prices rise, producers who could not previously compete will find that they can now make a profit in the chocolate business and will wish to supply. Moreover, previously existing firms may be able to expand output by working overtime, or buying fancy equipment not justified when selling chocolate at lower prices. In general, higher prices are

Why increases in price increase th quantity supplied

▼

needed to provide an incentive for firms to produce more chocolate. Other things equal, supply curves slope upward as we move to the right.

2   Just as we investigated the 'other things equal' along a demand curve, we now examine three categories of 'other things equal' along a supply curve. These categories are: technology available to producers, the cost of inputs (labour, machines, fuel, and raw materials), and government regulation. Along any particular supply curve, all of these are held constant. A change in any of these categories will shift the supply curve by changing the amount producers wish to supply at each price.

Technology

3   A supply curve is drawn for a given technology. An improvement in technology will shift the supply curve to the right since producers will be willing to supply a larger quantity than previously at each price. An improvement in cocoa refining makes it possible to produce more chocolate for any given total cost. So do improvements in mass production packaging techniques. Faster shipping and better refrigeration may lead to less wastage in spoiled cocoa beans. Each of these technological advances enables firms to supply more at each price.

4   As a determinant of supply, technology must be interpreted very broadly. It embraces all know-how about production methods, not merely the state of available machinery. In agriculture, the development of disease-resistant seeds is a technological advance. Improved weather forecasting might enable better timing of planting and harvesting. A technological advance is any idea that allows more output from the same inputs as before. Using the terminology of Chapter 1, a technological advance shifts the production possibility frontier outwards.

Input Costs

5   A particular supply curve is drawn for a given level of input prices. A reduction in input prices (lower wages, lower fuel costs) will induce firms to supply more output at each price, shifting the supply curve to the right. Higher input prices make production less attractive and shift the supply curve to the left. For example, if a late frost

destroys much of the cocoa crop, the ensuing scarcity will bid up the price of cocoa beans. Chocolate producers will then wish to supply less chocolate at each price than previously.

Government Regulation

6 In discussing technology we spoke only of technological advances. Once people have discovered a better production method they are unlikely subsequently to forget it. Government regulations can sometimes be viewed as imposing a technological change that is *adverse* for producers. If so, the effect of regulations will be to shift the supply curve to the left, reducing quantity supplied at each price.

7   More stringent safety regulations may prevent chocolate producers using the most productive process because it is quite dangerous to workers. Anti-pollution devices may raise the cost of making cars, and regulations to protect the environment may make it unprofitable for firms to extract surface mineral deposits which could have been cheaply quarried but whose extraction now requires expensive landscaping. Whenever government regulations prevent producers from selecting the production methods they would otherwise have chosen, the effect of these regulations is to shift the supply curve to the left.

The effect of government regulations

G. Check your understanding

1. Look at the first paragraph again. What words have the same meaning as:
● make or grow larger
● well-managed
● what is produced
● shown to be correct or reasonable

2. Look at paragraph 2 again. What words have the opposite meaning to:
● outputs
● finished

3. Look at paragraph 3 again. Can you explain the following:
● mass production
● packaging techniques
● refrigeration
● wastage

▼

4. Look at paragraph 4 again. What words have the same meaning as:
- made better
- includes
- only
- predicting

5. Look at paragraph 5 again. What words have the same meaning as:
- following
- persuade
- ruins completely

6. Look at paragraph 6 again. What words have the opposite meaning to:
- favourable
- removing
- probably

7. Look at paragraph 7 again. Which words correspond to these definitions:
- stop someone from doing something
- does not take money
- way in which something is made
- dig out of the ground
- to prevent harm or damage happening to someone or something

8. Now write short notes on:
- technology available to producers
- the cost of inputs
- government regulations

Use the information in the text and make sure your notes summarise what the writer has said.

H. Understanding discourse

A lecturer is giving some students a task to do before the end of the week. Note down what you must do.

_____

_____

_____

_____

_____

PRICE, INCOME AND DEMAND

A. Understanding a printed text (1)

The following text will introduce you to the topic of **the effect of price and income on demand quantities**. Look at the way it is divided into paragraphs. Pay attention to the table, figure and notes in the margin.

Now look at these questions:

1. From the heading, what do you expect this text to be about?
2. Do Table 4-1 and Figure 4-1 give the same information?

3. What example has the writer chosen to illustrate his points?
4. How many kinds of elasticity does the writer mention?
5. Which kind of elasticity does the writer explain in this text?

Read the passage through and find the answers to those questions. Remember, you do not have to understand every word to answer them.

4-1 THE PRICE RESPONSIVENESS OF DEMAND

1 The downward slope of the demand curve shows that quantity demanded increases as the price of a good falls. Frequently we need to know by how much the quantity demanded will increase. Table 4-1 presents some hypothetical numbers for the relation between ticket price and quantity demanded, other things equal. Figure 4-1 plots the demand curve, which happens to be a straight line in this example.

2   How should we measure the responsiveness of the quantity of tickets demanded to the price of tickets? One obvious measure is the *slope* of the demand curve. Each price cut of £1 leads to 8000 extra ticket sales per game. Suppose, however, that we wish to compare the price responsiveness of football ticket sales with the price responsiveness of the quantity of cars demanded: clearly, £1

The slope of the demand curve

TABLE 4-1
THE DEMAND FOR FOOTBALL TICKETS

PRICE (£/ticket)	QUANTITY OF TICKETS DEMANDED (thousands/game)
12.50	0
10.00	20
7.50	40
5.00	60
2.50	80
0	100

▼

FIGURE 4-1 THE DEMAND FOR FOOTBALL TICKETS. For given prices of related goods and consumer incomes, higher ticket prices reduce the quantity of tickets demanded.

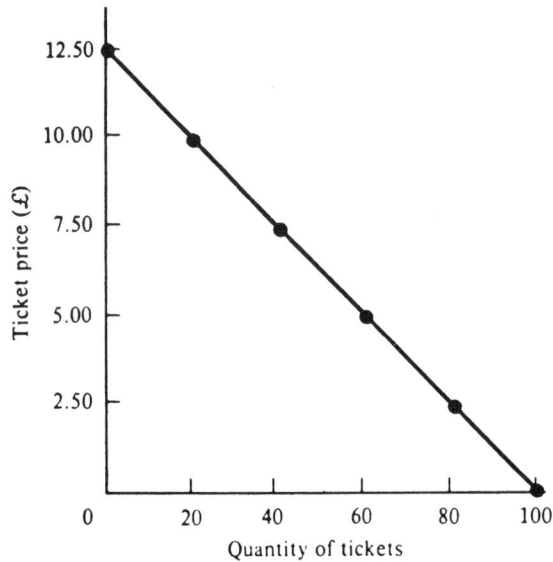

is a trivial cut in the price of a car and will have a negligible effect on the quantity of cars demanded.

3   In Chapter 2 we argued that when commodities are measured in different units it is often best to examine the percentage change, which is unit-free. This suggests that we think about the effect of a 1 per cent price cut on the quantity of cars and football tickets demanded. Similarly, it is not the absolute number of cars or tickets we should examine but the percentage change in quantity demanded. Not only does this solve the problem of comparing things measured in different quantity units, it also takes account of the size of the market. Presumably an extra sale of 8000 tickets is more important when ticket sales are 4000 than when they number 40 000.

4   Thus we reach the definition of the price elasticity of demand, which economists use to measure responsiveness to price changes.

> The *price elasticity of demand* is the percentage change in the quantity of a good demanded divided by the corresponding percentage change in its price.

Although we shall shortly introduce other demand elasticities – the cross price elasticity and the income elasticity – the (own) price elasticity is

Percentage change

Price elasticity of demand

perhaps the most frequently used of the three. Whenever economists speak of *the* demand elasticity they mean the price elasticity of demand as we have defined it above.

5   If a 1 per cent price increase reduces the quantity demanded by 2 per cent, the demand elasticity is -2. Because the quantity *falls* 2 per cent, we express this as a change of -2 per cent, then divide by the price change of 1 per cent (a price rise) to obtain -2. If a price fall of 4 per cent increases the quantity demanded by 2 per cent, the demand elasticity is $-\frac{1}{2}$, since the quantity change of 2 per cent is divided by the price change of -4 per cent. Since demand curves slope down, we are either dividing a positive percentage change in quantity (a quantity rise) by a negative percentage change in price (a price fall), or dividing a negative percentage change in quantity (a quantity fall) by a positive percentage change in price (a price rise). The price elasticity of demand tells us about movements along a demand curve and the demand elasticity must be a negative number.[1]

[1] For further brevity, economists sometimes omit the minus sign. It is easier to say the demand elasticity is 2 than to say it is -2. Whenever the price elasticity of demand is expressed as a positive number, it should be understood (unless there is an explicit warning to the contrary) that a minus sign should be added. Otherwise, we should be implying that demand curves slope upwards, a rare but not unknown phenomenon.

How to calculate demand elasticity

B. Check your understanding

Now read the text carefully, looking up any new items in a dictionary or reference book. Then answer the following questions:

1. What does Table 4-1 show?

2. What is the first measure the writer suggests?

3. What is the effect of a £1 price cut on football ticket sales?

4. Does the same price cut have the same effect on car sales?

5. In what circumstances do you examine the percentage change?

6. What problem does this solve?

7. How do economists use the price elasticity of demand?

8. Can you explain in your own words the definition of the price elasticity of demand?

9. Which is the commonest of the three demand elasticities?

10. Can you explain in your own words how to calculate demand elasticity?

▼

C. Increase your vocabulary

1. Look at the first paragraph again and say what words have the same meaning as:
- rarely
- upward
- crooked

2. Look at paragraph 2 again. What words have the same meaning as:
- not significant or important
- clear; easily seen or understood
- of small value or importance

3. Look at paragraph 3 again. Can you explain the following:
- different units
- percentage change
- unit-free
- absolute number

4. Look at paragraph 4 again. What words have the same meaning as:
- every time that
- in the near future
- in this way

5. Look at paragraph 5 and the footnote again. What words have the opposite meaning to:
- positive
- implicit
- include
- length

D. Check your grammar

DESCRIBING

1. Shorten the following sentences without changing their meaning, like this:

Nobody likes *prices which are constantly rising*.
Nobody likes *constantly rising prices*.

- A demand curve which slopes.
- John is a person who works very hard.
- We must develop a policy which fixes prices better.
- Interest rates which rise will damp down demand.
- An economy which is rapidly expanding can get out of control.
- Let us look at the information which corresponds to this in tabular form.

2. Shorten the following sentences without changing their meaning, like this:

The quantity which we require is 5000 units.
The required quantity is 5000 units.

- A demand curve which has been drawn inaccurately.
- A price which has been fixed.
- We can see changes in the prices of goods which are related to each other.
- She is a person who has changed since her examination results.
- The prices which we have been given should be seen as hypothetical.
- If we don't use a model which has been simplified we shall get bogged down.
- Ours is a company which is managed well.
- An economy which is poorly run leads to problems in society.
- That is a theory which is now out of date.
- On the evidence available, that is a conclusion which is not justified.

E. Understanding a lecture

You are now going to hear part of a lecture, divided into short sections to help you understand it. As you listen, answer the questions below.

Section 1
● What is the lecturer going to talk about?

● Which columns reproduce the data from Table 4-1?

(1) PRICE (£/ticket)	(2) QUANTITY OF TICKETS DEMANDED (thousands/game)	(3) PRICE ELASTICITY OF DEMAND
12.50	0	$-\infty$
10.00	20	-4
7.50	40	-1.5
5.00	60	-0.67
2.50	80	-0.25
0	100	0

TABLE 4-2 ▬▬▬▬
THE PRICE ELASTICITY OF DEMAND FOR FOOTBALL TICKETS

Section 2
Are these statements correct or incorrect?
● Price elasticity of demand is calculated by considering the effects of price cuts. ☐
● 20,000 tickets is the quantity that corresponds to a price of £10.00. ☐
● In this example, a 25% price cut leads to a 100% increase in demand. ☐

Section 3
● Note down how the answer -4 is arrived at.

● The sign the lecturer explains is /
  The sign / means (a) multiplied by ☐
                 (b) minus ☐
                 (c) divided by ☐
                 (d) plus ☐

Section 4
● Is this statement correct or incorrect?
  Other elasticities are not calculated in this way. ☐
● Note down how other elasticities are calculated.

Section 5
● What is the demand elasticity at a price of £12.50?

● Is this statement correct or incorrect?
  When you divide a positive number by 0 you get plus infinity. ☐

- Complete the definition the lecturer gives
  Demand elasticity is high when _____
- Complete the definition the lecturer gives
  Demand elasticity is low when _____
- Is this statement correct or incorrect?
  When economists use the words 'high' and 'low' they pay no attention to the minus sign. □

2. Now wind the cassette back to the beginning of the lecture and listen to it again. This time, instead of answering questions, take notes. The questions you have already answered will help you do this. When you have listened to the whole of the lecture, you will be asked to give a short oral summary of it. So make sure you note down the important points.

3. You should also write a summary of the lecture, based on your notes.

F. Understanding a printed text (2)

Read the following text carefully, looking up anything you do not understand.

Elastic and Inelastic Demand

Elastic and inelastic demand

1 Although elasticity typically falls as we move down the demand curve, an important dividing line occurs at the demand elasticity of -1.

Demand is *elastic* if the price elasticity is more negative than -1. Demand is *inelastic* if the price elasticity lies between -1 and 0.

In Table 4-2 demand is elastic at all prices of £7.50 and above and inelastic at all prices of £5.00 and below. If the demand elasticity is exactly -1, we say that demand is *unit-elastic*.

Unit-elastic demand

2 Later in this section we show that a cut in prices raises revenue from football ticket sales if demand for football tickets is elastic but lowers revenue if demand is inelastic. Whether or not demand is elastic is the key piece of information required in setting tube fares in the example of Chapter 2 and in setting the price of football tickets in the example we are currently studying.

High and low demand elasticities

3 Although the price elasticity of demand typically changes as we move along demand curves, economists frequently talk of goods with high or low demand elasticities. For example, they will say that the demand for oil is price-inelastic (price changes have only a small effect on quantity demanded) but the demand for foreign holidays is price-elastic (price changes have a large effect on quantity demanded). Such statements implicitly

refer to parts of the demand curve corresponding to prices (adjusted for inflation) that are typically charged for these goods or services. They do not necessarily describe the demand elasticity at points on the demand curve corresponding to real prices which have never been observed historically.

The Determinants of Price Elasticity

4 What determines whether the price elasticity of demand for a good is high (say, − 5) or low (say, −0.5)? Ultimately the answer must be sought in consumer tastes. If it is considered socially essential to own a television, higher television prices may have little effect on quantity demanded. If televisions are considered a frivolous luxury, the demand elasticity will be much higher. Psychologists and sociologists may be able to explain more fully than economists why tastes are as they are. Nevertheless, as economists, we can identify some considerations likely to affect consumer responses to changes in the price of a good. *The most important consideration is the ease with which consumers can substitute another good that fulfils approximately the same function.*

5 Consider two extreme cases. Suppose first that the price of all cigarettes is raised 1 per cent, perhaps because the cigarette tax has been raised. Do you expect the quantity of cigarettes demanded to fall by 5 per cent or by 0.5 per cent? Probably the latter. People who can easily quit smoking have already done so. A few smokers may try to cut down but this effect is unlikely to be large. In contrast, suppose the price of one particular brand of cigarettes is increased by 1 per cent, all other brand prices remaining unchanged. We should now expect a much larger quantity response from buyers. With so many other brands available at unchanged prices, consumers will switch away from the more expensive brand to other brands that basically fulfil the same function of nicotine provision. For a particular cigarette brand the demand elasticity could be quite high.

6 Ease of substitution implies a high demand elasticity for a particular good. In fact, our example suggests a general rule. The more narrowly we define a commodity (a particular brand of cigarette rather than cigarettes in general, or oil rather than energy as a whole), the larger will be the price elasticity of demand.

Consumer tastes decide whether demand is high or low

The importance of ease of substitution

Measuring Price Elasticities

7 To illustrate these general principles we report estimates of price elasticities of demand in Table 4-3. The table confirms that the demand for general categories of basic commodities, such as fuel, food, or even household durable goods, is inelastic. As a category, only services such as haircuts, the theatre, and sauna baths, have an elastic demand. Households simply do not have much scope to alter the broad pattern of their purchases.

8 In contrast, there is a much wider variation in the demand elasticities for narrower definitions of commodities. Even then, the demand for some commodities, such as dairy produce, is very inelastic. However, particular kinds of services such as entertainment and catering have a much more elastic demand. Small changes in the relative price of restaurant meals and theatre tickets may lead households to switch in large numbers between eating out and going to the theatre, whereas the demand for getting out of the house on a Saturday evening may be relatively insensitive to the price of all Saturday night activities taken as a whole.

TABLE 4-3

ESTIMATES OF PRICE ELASTICITIES OF DEMAND IN THE UK

GOOD (GENERAL CATEGORY)	DEMAND ELASTICITY	GOOD (NARROWER CATEGORY)	DEMAND ELASTICITY
Fuel and light	−0.47		
Food	−0.52	Dairy produce	−0.05
Alcohol	−0.83	Bread and cereals	−0.22
Durables	−0.89	Entertainment	−1.40
Services	−1.02	Expenditure abroad	−1.63
		Catering	−2.61

Sources: The left-hand column is taken from John Muellbauer, 'Testing the Barten Model of Household Composition Effects and the Cost of Children', *Economic Journal*, September, 1977, Table 7. The right-hand column is taken from Angus Deaton, 'The Measurement of Income and Price Elasticities', *European Economic Review*, Volume 6, 1975.

G. Check your understanding

1. Look at the first paragraph again. Is this statement correct or incorrect?
● Demand is unit-elastic when the price is £5.00. □

2. Look at paragraph 2 again. What words have the same meaning as:
● at the moment
● income
● reduces

3. Look at paragraph 3 again. Are these statements correct or incorrect?
- Oil is price-inelastic because price changes do not affect demand very much. ☐
- Holidays are price-elastic because their price influences whether people will buy them. ☐

4. Look at paragraph 4 again. What words have the same meaning as:
- not serious
- in the end
- replace with something similar
- carries out
- however, in spite of that

5. Look at paragraph 5 again. Are these statements correct or incorrect?
- The writer expects people to buy the same amount of cigarettes whatever the price. ☐
- People are likely to change their brand if its price rises when other brands keep the same price. ☐

6. Look at paragraph 6 again. Is this statement correct or incorrect?
- Price elasticity of demand will be greater if a wide range of commodities is considered. ☐

7. Look at paragraphs 7 and 8 again. Using the information given there, write your own explanation of Table 4-3.

_____

_____

_____

_____

H. Understanding discourse

Listen to a lecturer giving some students instructions about examinations. Note down what you must do.

_____

_____

_____

_____

_____

UNIT 10

A. Understanding a printed text (1)

The following text will introduce you to the topic of the theory of **consumer choice**. Look at the way it is divided into sections and paragraphs. Pay attention to the table, figure and notes in the margin.

Now look at these questions:

1. What is the writer's purpose in the first paragraph?

2. From the main heading, what do you expect this text to be about?
3. What is dealt with in the first section?
4. What is dealt with in the second section?
5. What is dealt with in the third section?

Read the passage through and find the answers to those questions. Remember, you do not have to understand every word to answer them.

What the model of consumer behaviour does

1 In previous chapters we have learned to use demand curves to represent consumer behaviour. The properties of these demand curves may usefully be summarized by own price, cross price, and income elasticities of demand. In this chapter we go behind these measures of demand by building a model of consumer behaviour. The model of consumer choice explains how buyers reconcile what they would like to do, as described by their tastes or preferences, and what the market will allow them to do, as described by their incomes and the prices of different goods. The model allows us to predict how consumers

will respond to changes in market conditions. It helps to make sense of the price and income elasticities examined in Chapter 4.

5-1 THE THEORY OF CONSUMER CHOICE

The four elements of the model

2 The model has four elements which describe both the consumer and the market environment:

1 The given income that the consumer can spend
2 The prices at which goods can be bought
3 The consumer's tastes, which rank different combinations or bundles of goods according to the satisfaction they yield the consumer
4 The behavioural assumption that consumers do the best they can for themselves. Of the possible consumption bundles that can be purchased out of a given income, the consumer picks the bundle that maximizes his or her own satisfaction.

3 Each of these elements in the model requires detailed discussion.

The Budget Constraint

4 Together, elements (1) and (2) define the consumer's budget constraint.

The *budget constraint* describes the different bundles that the consumer can afford.

Budget constraint

Which bundles are feasible, or can be afforded, depends on two factors: the consumer's income and the prices of different goods.

5   Consider a student with a weekly budget (income, allowance, or grant) of £50 which can be spent on meals or films.[1] Each meal costs £5 and each film £10. What combination of meals and films can the student afford to buy? Completely going without films, the student can spend £50 on 10 meals at £5

---

[1] When there are more than two goods, we can think of 'films' as standing for 'all goods other than meals'.

each. Completely going without meals, the student can buy 5 cinema tickets at £10 each. Between these two extremes lies a range of combinations of meals and films that together cost exactly £50. These combinations are called the budget constraint.

6   Thus, the budget constraint shows the *maximum* affordable quantity of one good given the quantity of the other good that is being purchased.[2] Table 5-1 shows the budget constraint for the student in our example. Each row of the table shows an affordable consumption bundle. For example, row 4 shows that 6 meals (costing £30) and 2 films (costing £20) use up all available income. Other rows are calculated in the same way.

What the budget constraint shows

7   Table 5-1 shows the *trade-off* the student must make between meals and films. Higher quantities of meals require lower quantities of films. For a given income, the budget constraint shows how much of one good must be sacrificed to obtain larger quantities of the other good. It is because there is a trade-off that the student must make a *choice between* meals and films.

The Budget Line

8 It is useful to depict the budget constraint of Table 5-1 as a *budget line*. Plotting the data of Table 5-1, the budget line in Figure 5-1 again shows the

What the budget line shows

---

[2] We assume that all income is spent on goods. There is no saving.

TABLE 5-1

ALTERNATIVE AFFORDABLE CONSUMPTION BASKETS

QUANTITY OF MEALS (Q_M)	SPENDING ON MEALS (£5 × Q_M)	QUANTITY OF FILMS (Q_f)	SPENDING ON FILMS (£10 × Q_f)
0	0	5	50
2	10	4	40
4	20	3	30
6	30	2	20
8	40	1	10
10	50	0	0

maximum combinations of meals and films that the student can purchase out of available income.

How the budget line is determined

9   The position and shape of the budget line are determined by its end points A and F, which have a simple economic interpretation. Point A shows the maximum quantity of films (5) that the budget will purchase if the student goes without meals: £50 buys at most 5 tickets at £10 each. Point F shows that £50 buys at most 10 meals at £5 each if the student goes without films. The budget line joins up points A and F. Intermediate points on the line such as B and C show more balanced purchases of meals and films.

The use of the budget line

10   The budget line is a convenient way to examine the trade-off between meals and films. The slope of the budget line indicates how many meals must be sacrificed to get another film. Moving from point F to point E reduces the quantity of meals from 10 to 8 but increases the quantity of films from 0 to 1. This trade-off between meals and films is constant along the budget line. Giving up two meals at £5 each always provides the extra £10 to buy an additional cinema ticket.

The importance of prices

11   We now see the crucial role of prices. It is because film tickets cost twice as much as meals that two meals must be sacrificed to purchase another film ticket. If films cost three times as much as meals it would be necessary to sacrifice three meals to pay for one extra film. *The slope of the budget line depends only on the ratio of the prices of the two goods.* The slope of a line is the change in the vertical distance divided by the corresponding change in the horizontal distance. In Figure 5-1 the slope of the budget line is $-\frac{1}{2}$. A positive change of 1 film must be divided by the corresponding negative change of -2 meals.

The general rule

12   This example illustrates the general rule

Slope of the budget line $= -P_H/P_V$ (1)

where P_H is the price of the good whose quantity is measured on the horizontal axis and P_V is the

FIGURE 5-1 THE BUDGET LINE. The budget line shows the maximum combinations of goods that the consumer can afford, given income and the prevailing prices. Points such as *B* and *C*, on the budget line *AF*, use up the entire consumer budget. Points such as *G*, above the budget line, are unaffordable. Points such as *K*, inside the budget line, would allow additional consumption of at least one good.

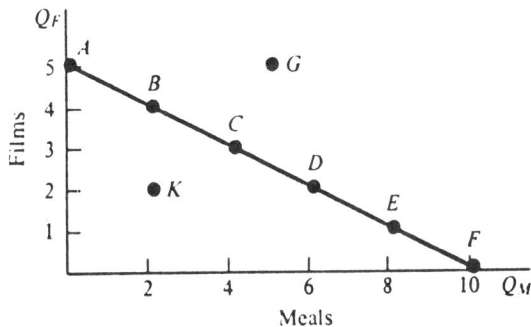

price of the good whose quantity is measured on the vertical axis. In our example, the price of meals P_H is £5 and the price of films P_V is £10. Formula (1) confirms that the slope of the budget line is $-\frac{1}{2}$ and the minus sign reminds us that there is a trade-off. We have to *give up* one good to get more of the other good.

13   Thus, the two end-points of the budget line (here, *A* and *F*) show how much of each good the budget will buy if the other good is not purchased at all. The slope of the budget line joining these end-points, depends only on the *relative* prices of the two goods.

14   Any point above the budget line (such as *G* in Figure 5-1) is unaffordable. The budget line shows the maximum quantity of one good that can be afforded, given the quantity purchased of the other good and given the budget available for spending. Given an income of £50, the point *G* is out of reach since it requires £25 to buy 5 meals and £50 to buy 5 cinema tickets. Points such as *K*, which lie inside the budget line, leave some income unspent. The point *K* requires £10 for meals and £20 for films leaving £20 unspent. The student could use this £20 to buy 4 extra meals (moving from *K* to *D* without sacrificing films) or to buy 2 extra film tickets (moving from *K* to *B* without sacrificing meals). Only on the budget line is there a trade-off where the student must choose *between* films and meals.

The budget line interpreted

B. Check your understanding

Now read the text carefully, looking up any new items in a dictionary or reference book. Then answer the following questions:

1. What is reconciled by the model of consumer choice?

2. What does the writer assume about how consumers behave?

3. What does the consumer's ability to buy depend on?

4. On what assumption is Table 5-1 based?

5. What does the budget line in Figure 5-1 show?

6. How are the position and shape of the budget line determined?

7. What is constant along the budget line?

8. What does the slope of the budget line depend on?

9. Why is point G in Figure 5-1 unaffordable?

10. At point K, has the student spent all his/her money?

C. Increase your vocabulary

1. Look at the first paragraph again and say what words correspond to these definitions:
- special qualities that belong to something
- the way someone acts
- say in advance
- people's likings or preferences

2. Look at paragraphs 2 and 3 again. What words have the same meaning as:
- makes the most of
- put, arrange in order
- surroundings
- give
- chooses

3. Look at paragraph 4 again. What words have the opposite meaning to:
- not possible
- apart

4. Look at paragraph 5 again. Can you explain what the writer means by:
- these two extremes
- budget constraint

5. Look at paragraph 6 again. What words have the opposite meaning to:
- cannot be bought
- minimum

6. Look at paragraph 7 again. What words have the same meaning as:
- get
- given up

7. Look at paragraph 8 again. Find alternative words you could use in the text instead of:
- useful
- depict
- purchase

8. Look at paragraph 9 again. Can you explain the points:
- A
- F
- B
- C

9. Look at paragraph 10 again. What does the writer mean by:
- trade-off

10. Look at paragraph 11 again. What words have the same meaning as:
- existing at the time
- a minimum of
- whole

11. Look at paragraph 12 again. Using the information in the paragraph, can you explain:
- $-P_H/P_V$

12. Look at paragraph 13 again. Can you explain the words:
- end-point
- relative prices

13. Look at paragraph 14 again. What words have the same meaning as:
- beyond one's financial means
- to hand, in one's possession

D. Check your grammar

Complete the following paragraph using the right preposition.

Income elasticities are key pieces . . . . information . . . . forecasting the pattern . . . . consumer demand as the economy grows and people become richer. Suppose we think that, ... average, incomes will grow . . . . 3 per cent per annum . . . . the next five years. Given the estimates . . . . Table 4-11, a 15 per cent change . . . . incomes will reduce the demand . . . . tobacco . . . . 7.5 per cent, but will increase the demand . . . . drinks . . . . 39 per cent. The growth prospects . . . . these two industries are very different. These forecasts will affect decisions . . . . firms about whether or not to build new factories and projections . . . . governments . . . . tax revenue . . . . cigarettes and drinks.

E. Understanding a lecture

You are now going to hear part of a lecture, divided into short sections to help you understand it. As you listen, answer the questions below:

Section 1
- Note down the subject that the students have been studying.

- Note down the particular point the lecturer is going to talk about.

Section 2
- How many assumptions is the lecturer going to make?

- Is this statement correct or incorrect?
  The students are not allowed to disagree with the lecturer. ☐
- Note down the definiton of 'utility' the lecturer gives you.

• According to the lecturer, consumers
  cannot decide between different bundles of goods. ☐
  will always say one bundle is as good as another. ☐
  can decide whether one bundle is better, worse or the same as another. ☐
  should not be consulted by economists. ☐

Section 4

• Note down the second assumption.

_____

Section 5

Are these statements correct or incorrect?
• Economists cannot handle 'bads'. ☐
• Note down how economists handle 'bads', if they do.

_____

Section 6

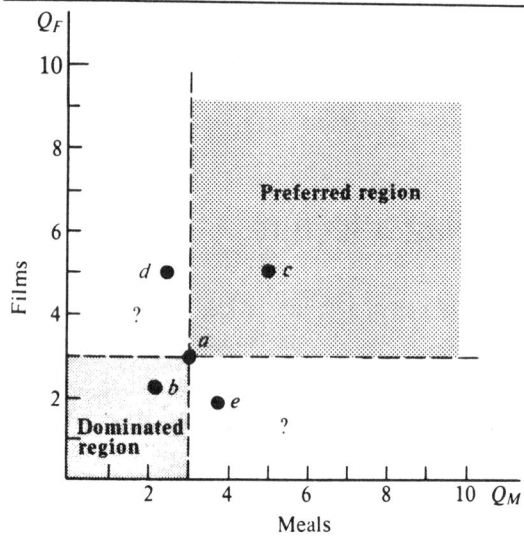

• What do the points a, b etc. represent?

_____

• Where do you start to draw the figure?

_____

• Then what do you do?

_____

Section 7

• Is this statement correct or incorrect?
  Point b is better than point c. ☐

Section 8————————————————————————————————
- Note down the term the lecturer wants you to.

_____

_____

Section 9————————————————————————————————
- Write down the definition of the term.

_____

_____

_____

_____

2. First, say what you think the lecturer means by the definition he has given you. Use the notes you have just made to help you.

3. Wind the cassette back to the beginning of the lecture and listen to it again. This time, instead of answering questions, take notes. When you have listened to the whole of the lecture, you will be asked to give a short oral summary of it. So make sure you note down the important points.

4. You should also write a summary of the lecture, based on your notes.

F. Understanding a printed text (2)

Do you remember the last lecture? The lecturer did not talk about his third assumption. Here is a handout he gave the students. Read the handout, looking up anything you do not understand.

> We now introduce the concept of the marginal rate of substitution of meals for films.
>> The *marginal rate of substitution* of meals for films is the quantity of films the consumer must sacrifice to increase the quantity of meals by one unit *without changing total utility.*
>
> Since consumers prefer more to less, an additional meal tends to increase utility. To hold utility constant, when one meal is added the consumer must simultaneously sacrifice some quantity of the other good (films). The marginal rate of susbstitution tells us how many films the consumer could exchange for an additional meal without changing total utility. The marginal rate of substitution must be a negative number: it is the ratio of a negative change in the quantity of films to the positive change in the quantity of meals when utility remains unaltered.

▼

Suppose the student begins with a bundle comprising 5 films and no meals. Having already seen 4 films that week, the student probably does not enjoy the fifth film very much. With no meals, the student is *very* hungry. The utility of this bundle is low: being so hungry, the student cannot really enjoy the films anyway. To obtain the same amount of utility the student could give up a lot of films in exchange for a little food. The marginal rate of substitution is a large negative number and we say that it is high.

Suppose instead that the student is consuming a large number of meals but seeing few films. To obtain the same amount of utility, the student will be reluctant to sacrifice much cinema attendance to gain yet another meal. The marginal rate of substitution is a small negative number and we say that it is low. When the ratio of films to meals is already high the marginal rate of substitution of meals for films is high. It makes sense to sacrifice abundant films for scarce meals. Conversely, when the ratio of films to meals is already low the marginal rate of substitution of meals for films is low. It does not make sense to sacrifice scarce films for yet more meals.

Economists believe that this common-sense reasoning about tastes or preferences is very robust. It will hold in a wide range of circumstances. Indeed, it is sufficiently plausible that it can become a general principle, the third assumption we need to make about consumer tastes. It is called the assumption of a diminishing marginal rate of substitution.

> Consumer tastes exhibit a *diminishing marginal rate of substitution* when, to hold utility constant, diminishing quantities of one good must be sacrificed to obtain successive equal increases in the quantity of the other good.

For example, our student might be indifferent between, that is, be equally happy with, bundle $X = (6$ films, 0 meals), bundle $Y = (3$ films, 1 meal), and bundle $Z = (2$ films, 2 meals). Beginning from bundle X, a move to Y sacrifices 3 films for 1 meal, but a further move from Y to Z sacrifices only 1 film for 1 extra meal. Such tastes satisfy the assumption of a diminishing marginal rate of substitution.

These three assumptions – that consumers prefer more to less, can rank alternative bundles according to the utility provided, and have tastes satisfying a diminishing marginal rate of substitution – are all we shall require. It is now convenient to show how tastes can be represented as *indifference curves*.

G. Check your understanding

1. Give a short, oral summary of what you think the text is about.

2. When you listened to the lecture, you predicted what the lecturer's definition meant. Now identify the points where your prediction is different from what the lecturer says.

3. Discuss these differences in your class.

H. Understanding discourse

A tutor is talking to a student, who is not studying in the way the tutor wants him to. Note down what the tutor thinks about the way the student is studying, and what she thinks the student should do.

_____

_____

_____

_____

_____

_____

_____

_____

2

T he following short test is for you to check whether you are learning the skills you will need to study Economics in English. It is for *your* information. It is *not* an examination. You may use a dictionary.

A. Reading

Read the following text and then answer the questions.

Representing Tastes as Indifference Curves

1 If we join up all the many points the student likes equally, we obtain an indifference curve.

What an indifference curve shows

An *indifference curve* shows all the consumption bundles which yield the same utility to the consumer.

Figure 5-3 shows three indifference curves labelled U_1U_1, U_2U_2, and U_3U_3.

2 Every point on U_2U_2 yields the same utility. Point C offers a lot of meals and few films, point B offers a more balanced quantity of meals and films, and point A offers many films but few meals. Because the consumer prefers more to less, *indifference curves must slope downwards*. Since more meals tend to increase utility, some films

Indifference curves must slope downwards

FIGURE 5-3 REPRESENTING CONSUMER TASTES BY INDIFFERENCE CURVES. Along each indifference curve, such as U_2U_2, consumer utility is constant. Since more is preferred to less, any point on a higher indifference curve, such as U_3U_3, is preferred to any point on a lower indifference curve. Indifference curves must slope downwards. Otherwise the consumer would have more of both goods and would be better off. Diminishing marginal rates of substitution imply that each indifference curve becomes flatter as we move along it to the right.

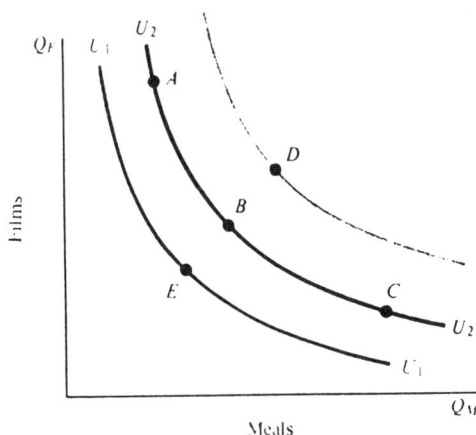

must simultaneously be sacrificed to hold utility constant.

3 *The slope of each indifference curve gets steadily flatter as we move to the right.* This follows immediately from the assumption of a diminishing marginal rate of substitution. At point A, where films are relatively abundant compared with meals, the consumer will sacrifice a lot c films to gain a little more food. At the point B, where films are less abundant relative to meals, the consumer will sacrifice a smaller quantity of films to gain the same additional quantity of meals. And at the point C the student now has so many meals that hardly any films will be sacrificed for additional meals. In fact, we now recognize that the marginal rate of substitution of meals for films is simply the slope of the indifference curve at the point from which we begin. These two properties of a single indifference curve – its downward slope and its steady flattening as we move to the right – follow directly from the assumptions that consumers prefer more to less and that their tastes satisfy the assumption of diminishing marginal rates of substitution.

4 Now consider the point D, which lies on a different indifference curve U_3U_3. Point D offers more of both goods than point B. Since consumers prefer more to less, utility at D must be higher than utility at B. By definition, all points on U_3U_3 yield the same utility. The difference between U_2U_2 and U_3U_3 is that every point on U_3U_3 yields more utility than every point on U_2U_2. Conversely, point E must yield less utility than point B since it offers less of both goods. Every point on U_1U_1 yields less utility than every point on U_2U_2.

5 Although in Figure 5-3 we have drawn only three indifference curves, we can imagine drawing in other indifference curves as well. As we move on to higher indifference curves we move to bundles that will be preferred. Higher indifference curves are better because the consumer prefers more to less.

6 You may be wondering if it is a coincidence that we have not drawn any indifference curves that cross each other. It is not: our assumptions guarantee that indifference curves cannot cross. Figure 5-4 shows why. Suppose the indifference curves UU and U'U' were to intersect. Since X and Y lie on the same indifference curve UU, the

The slope gets flatter as we move to the right

Why indifference curves have these properties

Indifference curves cannot cross

▼

103

consumer is indifferent between these points. But Y and Z both lie on the indifference curve U'U'. Hence the consumer is indifferent between Y and Z. Together these imply that the consumer is indifferent between X and Z. But this is impossible, since the consumer gets more of both goods at Z than at X. Hence intersecting indifference curves would violate our assumption that consumers prefer more to less. Our assumptions about consumer tastes rule out intersecting indifference curves.

FIGURE 5-4 INDIFFERENCE CURVES CANNOT INTERSECT. If indifference curves intersected, the consumer would be indifferent between X and Y, which both lie on the indifference curve UU, and between Y and Z, which both lie on the indifference curve U'U'. Hence the consumer would be indifferent between X and Z. Since Z offers more of both goods than X, this violates the assumption that consumers prefer more to less. Hence indifference curves cannot intersect.

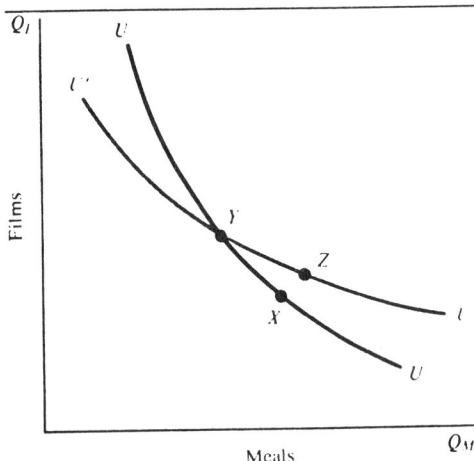

Answer these questions.

---

1. Look at paragraphs 1 and 2 again. What words have the same meaning as:
- given up
- at the same time
- getting less
- unchanging

---

2. Look at paragraph 3 again. Are these statements correct or incorrect?
- It is because of an assumption that indifference curves get flatter towards the right. ☐
- The consumer has fewer films at point A than at point B. ☐
- Note down the two properties of an indifference curve.

- Note down the two assumptions on which these properties are based.

3. Look at paragraphs 4 and 5 again. Is this statement correct or incorrect?

- Point D yields more utility than point E. □
  - Why are higher indifference curves preferred?

_____

4. Look at paragraph 6 again. Are these statements correct or incorrect?

- It is a matter of chance that indifference curves cannot cross. □
- The consumer cannot be indifferent between points X and Z. □

B. Writing

Read the following text. Then, using your own words, write a summary of it.

Utility Maximization and Consumer Choice

1 The budget line describes the affordable bundles given the consumer's market environment (the budget for spending and the price of different goods). The indifference map shows the tastes of the consumer. To complete the model, we add the behavioural assumption that *the consumer chooses the affordable bundle that maximizes his or her utility*.

2 The consumer cannot afford points that lie above the budget line and will never choose points that lie below the budget line. If the consumer begins at a point below the budget line, some income is unspent and it is possible to purchase more of one good without sacrificing any of the other good. Spending all the available budget and thereby moving on to the budget line must increase utility since the consumer prefers more to less.

3 Thus we know the consumer will select a point on the budget line. To determine which point on the budget line maximizes utility we need to think about the consumer's tastes. We expect our glutton to pick a point with more meals and less films than the point our film buff will select. We begin by showing in general how to use indifference curves to determine the bundle the consumer will choose. Then we confirm that our model of consumer choice can capture the different behaviour of the glutton and the film buff.

4 Figure 5-6 again shows the budget line AF for the student who has £50 to spend on films at £10 each and meals at £5 each. The indifference curves U_1U_1, U_2U_2, and U_3U_3 are part of the complete indifference map describing the student's tastes.

▼

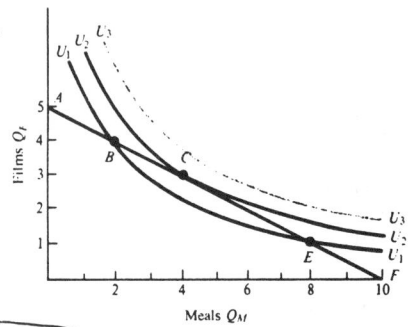

FIGURE 5-6 CONSUMER CHOICE IN ACTION. Points above the budget line AF are unaffordable. The consumer cannot reach the indifference curve U_3U_3. Points such as B and E are affordable but only allow the consumer to reach the indifference curve U_1U_1. The consumer will choose the point C to reach the highest possible indifference curve U_2U_2. At the chosen point C, the indifference curve and the budget line just touch and their slopes are equal.

point A, which must lie on a lower indifference curve (since indifference curves cannot intersect, the indifference curve through A must lie everywhere below the indifference curve U_1U_1). Similarly, the point F must lie on a lower indifference The student prefers any point on U_3U_3 to any point on U_2U_2, which in turn is preferred to any point on U_1U_1.

5   Since U_3U_3 lies everywhere above the budget line AF, all points on U_3U_3 are unattainable, however much the student would like to obtain this amount of utility. Suppose the student considers the attainable point B on the indifference curve U_1U_1. This will certainly be preferred to the curve than the point E and the student prefers E to F.

6   However, the student will chose neither the point B nor the point E. By moving to the point C he or she can reach a higher indifference curve and obtain more utility, so C is the point that the student will choose. Any other affordable point on the budget line will place the student on a lower indifference curve, and any indifference curve above U_2U_2 lies entirely above the budget line AF and involves bundles that are unaffordable given the budget constraint. The assumption that consumers choose the bundle that maximizes their utility given the affordable possibilities described by the budget line thus has the following simple implication: *the chosen bundle will be the point at which an indifference curve just touches the budget line.* Mathematicians would say that the budget line is *a tangent* to the indifference curve U_2U_2 at the point C. The budget line does not ever cross any higher indifference curve, such as U_3U_3 and crosses twice every lower indifference curve, such as U_1U_1. Point C describes the point of maximum utility given the budget constraint.

C. Listening

You will now hear part of a lecture. Listen to each section twice. After you have listened to each section for a second time, answer the questions below.

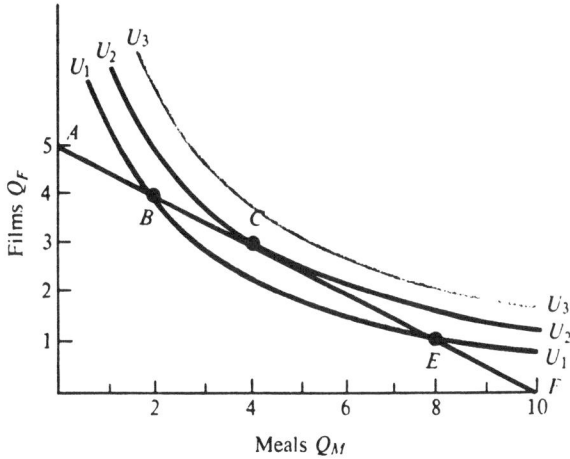

Meals Q_M

Section 1
Are these statements correct or incorrect?
- The lecturer is going to come to a different conclusion. ☐
- He is going to use an alternative way of reasoning. ☐

Complete the following sentence, using the same terms as the lecturer:
- The _____ of the budget line indicates a _____ between affordable quantities of meals and films that the _____ _____ will allow.

Section 2
Complete the following sentence, using the same terms as the lecturer:
- Point B shows how the consumer would trade meals for films to preserve a _____ _____ of _____.

Are these statements correct or incorrect?
- It is sensible to move to the left of point B. ☐
- A move to the left would take the student onto a higher indifference curve. ☐

Section 3
- Is this statement correct or incorrect?
  A move to the left of point E makes no sense. ☐

Section 4
- Is this statement correct or incorrect?
  Moves to the right of point B and to the left of point E both make sense. ☐

Section 5—————————————————————————————————

- Note down the general principle the lecturer explains.

  _____

  _____

  _____

  _____

Section 6—————————————————————————————————

- Note down why point C is significant.

  _____

  _____

  _____

  _____

A. Understanding a printed text (1)

The following text will introduce you to the topic of **output supply** – revenues, costs and profits. Look at the way it is divided into sections and paragraphs. Pay attention to the figure and notes in the margin.

Now look at these questions:

1. Look at the heading and say what you expect to find in the text.

2. How does the writer define profits?
3. What is the purpose of Figure 6-2?
4. What concept is raised in section 2?
5. What is the purpose of section 3?

Read the passage through and find the answers to those questions. Remember, you do not have to understand every word to answer them.

6-2 REVENUES, COSTS, AND PROFITS

1   A firm's *revenue* is the amount it earns by selling goods or services in a given period such as a year. The firm's *costs* are the expenses incurred in producing goods or services during the period. *Profits* are the excess of revenues over costs.

Thus we can write

Profits = revenues – cost   **(1)**

How to calculate profits

Although these ideas are simple, in practice the calculation of revenues, costs, and profits for a large business is complicated. Otherwise we would not need so many accountants. We begin with a simple example.

2   Rent-a-Person is a firm that hires people whom it then rents out to other firms that need temporary workers. Rent-a-Person charges £10 per hour per worker but pays its workers only £7 per hour. During 1987 it rented 100 000 hours of labour. Business expenses, including leasing an office, buying advertising space, and paying telephone bills, came to £200 000. Figure 6-2 shows the *income statement* or *profit-and-loss account* for 1987. Profits or net income before taxes were £100 000. Taxes to central government (corporation tax) plus taxes to local government (rates assessed on some of the property the firm owned) came to £25 000. Rent-a-Person's after-tax profits in 1987 were £75 000.

What Figure 6-2 shows

3   Now we can discuss some of the complications in calculating profits.

Outstanding Bills

4 People do not always pay their bills immediately. At the end of 1987, Rent-a-Person has not been paid for all the workers it hired out during the year. On the other hand, it has not paid its telephone bill for December. From an economic viewpoint, the right definition of revenues and costs relates to the activities carried out during the year whether or not payments have yet been made.

5   This distinction between economic revenues and costs and actual receipts and payments raises the important concept of cash flow.

> A firm's *cash flow* is the net amount of money actually received during the period.

Profitable firms may still have a poor cash flow, for example when customers are slow to pay their bills.

6   Part of the problem of running a business is that cash flow at the beginning is bound to be slow. Set up costs must be incurred before revenues

---

FIGURE 6-2
Rent-a-Person
Income Statement
For the Year Ending 31 December 1987

Revenue		£1 000 000
(100 000 hours rented out at £10 per hour)		
Deduct expenses (costs)		
Wages paid to people rented out	£700 000	
Advertising	50 000	
Office rent	50 000	
Wages for office workers	80 000	
Other office expenses	20 000	
		900 000
Net income (profits) before taxes		£100 000
Taxes paid		25 000
Net income (profits) after taxes		£75 000

---

start to flow in. That is why firms need financial capital to start the business. If the business prospers, revenues will build up and eventually there will be a healthy cash inflow.

Capital and Depreciation

7   *Physical capital* is the machinery, equipment, and buildings used in production.

Rent-a-Person owns little physical capital. Instead, it rents office space, typewriters, and desks. In practice, businesses frequently buy physical capital. Economists use 'capital' to denote goods not entirely used up in the production process during the period. Buildings and lorries are capital because they can be used again in the next year. Electricity is not a capital good because it is used up entirely during the period. Economists also use the terms 'durable goods' or 'physical assets' to describe capital goods.

8   How should the cost of a capital good such as typewriters be treated in calculating profits and costs? The essential idea is that it is the cost of *using* rather than *buying* a piece of capital equipment that should be treated as part of the firm's costs within the year. If Rent-a-Person leases all its capital equipment, its costs include merely the rentals paid in leasing capital goods.

9   Suppose however that Rent-a-Person buys eight typewriters at the beginning of the year for £1000 each. It should *not count* £8000 as the cost of typewriters in calculating costs and profits for that year. Rather, the cost should be calculated as the reduction in the value of the typewriters over the year. Suppose the wear-and-tear on the typewriters over the year has reduced their value from £1000 to £700 each. The economic cost of the use of eight typewriters over the year is £2400 (8 × £300). This amount of depreciation is the cost during the year.

> *Depreciation* is the loss in value resulting from the use of machinery during the period.

The cost during the period of using a capital good is the depreciation or loss of value of that good, not its purchase price.

Depreciation

10   The existence of depreciation again leads to a difference between economic profits and cash flow. When a capital good is first purchased there is a large cash outflow, much larger than the depreciation cost of using the good during the first year. Profits may be high but cash flow low. However, in subsequent years the firm makes no further cash outlay, having already paid for the capital goods, but must still calculate depreciation as an economic cost since the resale value of goods is reduced still further. Cash flow will now be higher than economic profit.

The difference between economic profits and cash flow

11   The consequence of treating depreciation rather than purchase price as the true economic cost is thus to spread the initial cost over the life of the capital good; but that is not the reason for undertaking the calculation in this way. Rent-a-Person could always have sold its typewriters for £5600 after one year, restricting its costs to £2400. The fact that the firm chose to keep them for re-use in the next year indicates that the latter strategy is even more profitable. Hence the true economic cost of *using* the typewriters in the first year can be at most £2400.

B. Check your understanding

Now read the text carefully, looking up any new items in a dictionary or reference book. Then answer the following questions:

1. Why do we need a great many accountants?

2. How much did Rent-a-Person pay in wages in 1987?

3. What was Rent-a-Person's pre-tax profits?

4. What is cash flow?

5. Why does a firm need financial capital to start its business?

6. Why is electricity not a capital good?

7. How should you treat the cost of a car in a firm's accounts?

8. What is depreciation?

9. Must you have a good cash flow in order to make a high profit?

10. What is the effect of using depreciation rather than purchase price?

C. Increase your vocabulary

1. Look at the first paragraph again. Can you explain the terms: ·
- revenue
- costs
- profits

2. Look at paragraphs 2 and 3 again. What words correspond to these definitions?
- to make a regular payment for the use of something
- to pay rent for the use of something over a fixed period of time
- to obtain the services of someone in exchange for payment
- decide or fix the amount of something

3. Look at paragraph 4 again and say what these words refer to:
- line 3: it
- line 4: it

4. Look at paragraph 5 again. Can you explain the terms:
- actual receipts
- net amount

5. Look at paragraph 6 again. What words have the same meaning as:
- makes money, does well financially
- certain
- brought on oneself

6. Look at paragraph 7 again. What words have the same meaning as:
- lasting
- wholly
- often

7. Look at paragraph 8 again. Write a sentence showing you know the meaning of the words:
- capital good
- essential
- treat
- merely
- rental

8. Look at paragraph 9 again. Can you explain the words:
- wear-and-tear
- loss of value
- purchase price

9. Look at paragraph 10 again. What words have the opposite meaning to:
- revenue, income
- inflow
- preceding

10. Look at paragraph 11 again. What words have the same meaning as:
- for this reason, from here
- carrying out (a piece of work)
- overall plan
- limiting

D. Check your grammar

SENTENCE AND PARAGRAPH WRITING

Make complete sentences out of the following notes, putting the verb in brackets in the right tense. Then arrange each group of sentences into a paragraph. Make sure that the sentences follow each other logically and that the paragraphs make sense.

1. ● production/fact/time/in (take)

_____

● goods/stock/the/inventories/by/sales/in/future/firm/for (be; hold)

_____

● inventories/demand/firms/future/to meet (hold)

_____

● production/instantaneous/if (be), as/firms/to meet/orders/they (can produce; arise)

2. ● year/and/it/one million/during/950,000/new/the/cars (produce; sell)

_____

● profit/how/the/calculation/this? (complicate)

_____

● beginning/stock/100,000/of/at/the Rover Group/cars/the/a 1987/of (suppose; have)

_____

● for/these/available/cars/and/sale (complete; be)

_____

● 950,000/the/revenues/sale/of/from/cars (accrue)

_____

● one million/costs/on/or/actually/sales/950,000/of/cars/the? (should base; make)

_____

● end/inventories/finished cars/by/its/the/of/150,000/to/year/of/the (rise)

_____

3. ● cars/capital/itself/like/stocks/the/50,000/firm/the/to/for (add; be; make)

_____

● to/the/950,000/that/answer/actually/cars/the/costs (be; should relate; sell)

_____

● the/period/available/sale/in/for/they/following (be)

_____

E. Understanding a lecture

You will now hear part of a lecture, divided into short sections to help you understand it. As you listen, answer the questions below.

Section 1

● Note down what document the lecturer expects the students to understand.

● Note down what document the lecturer is going to talk about.

● Note down what this document shows.

Section 2

● Note down what the balance sheet lists.

● What does this provide?

FIGURE 6-3
Snark International
Balance Sheet
31 December 1987

ASSETS		LIABILITIES	
Cash	£40 000	Accounts payable	£90 000
Accounts receivable	70 000	Salaries payable	50 000
Inventories	100 000	Mortgage from insurance	
Factory building		company	150 000
(original value £250 000)	200 000	Bank loan	60 000
Other equipment			———
(original value £300 000)	180 000		350 000
		Net worth	240 000
	———		———
	590 000		590 000

Section 3

● Note down what is meant by 'accounts receivable'.

● Why is the value of the factory building and other equipment not shown at its original cost?

Section 4

● Note down what is meant by 'accounts payable'.

● Why has Snark got a bank loan?

- Note down the term the lecturer tells you to.

_____

- What does this term represent?

_____

_____

Section 5—————————————————————————————————
- Note down why net worth is shown as a liability.

_____

_____

Section 6—————————————————————————————————
- Complete the following sentence with the term the lecturer uses.
  If you want to buy the company you should make a _____
- The lecturer gives two examples of intangibles. What are they?

_____

- What do economists call these intangibles?

_____

_____

2. Now wind the cassette back to the beginning of the lecture and listen to it again. This time, instead of answering questions, take notes. When you have listened to the whole of the lecture, you will be asked to give a short oral summary of it. So make sure you note down the important points.

3. You should also write a summary of the lecture, based on your notes.

F. Understanding a printed text (2)

Read the following text carefully, looking up anything you do not understand.

Earnings
1   Finally, we must consider what the firm does with its profits after taxes. It can pay them out to shareholders as dividends, or keep them in the firm as retained earnings.

> *Retained earnings* are the part of after-tax profits that is ploughed back into the business rather than paid out to shareholders as dividends.

Retained earnings

Retained earnings affect the balance sheet. If they are kept as cash or used to purchase new equipment, they increase the asset side of the balance sheet. Alternatively, they may be used to reduce the firm's liabilities, for example by repaying the bank loan. Either way, the firm's net worth is increased.

How retained earnings can be used

Opportunity Cost and Accounting Costs

2 The income statement and the balance sheet of a company provide a useful guide to how that company is doing. We have already hinted that economists and accountants do not always take the same view of costs and profits. Whereas the accountant is chiefly interested in describing the actual receipts and payments of a company, the economist is chiefly interested in the role of costs and profits as determinants of the firm's supply decision, the allocation of resources to particular activities. Accounting methods can be seriously misleading in two ways.

3 Economists identify the cost of using a resource not as the payment actually made but as its opportunity cost.

> *Opportunity cost* is the amount lost by not using the resource (labour or capital) in its best alternative use.

To show that this is the right measure of costs, given the questions economists wish to study, we give two examples.

4 Any persons working in their own businesses should take into account the cost of their own labour time spent in the business. A self-employed sole trader might draw up an income statement such as Figure 6-2, find that profits were £20 000 per annum, and conclude that this business was a good thing. But this conclusion neglects the opportunity cost of the individual's labour, the money that could have been earned by working elsewhere. If that individual could have earned a salary of £25 000 working for someone else, being self-employed is actually *losing* the person £5000 per annum even though the business is making an accounting profit of £20 000. If we wish to understand the incentives that the market provides to guide people towards particular occupations, we must use the economic concept of opportunity cost, not the accounting concept of actual payments. Including the opportunity cost of £25 000 in the income statement would quickly convince the individual that the business was not such a good idea.

5 The second place where opportunity cost must be counted is with respect to capital. Somebody has put up the money to start the business. In calculating accounting profits, no cost is attached to the use of owned (as opposed to borrowed) financial capital. This financial capital could have

been used elsewhere, in an interest-bearing bank account or perhaps to buy shares in a different company. The opportunity cost of that financial capital is included in the *economic* costs of the business but not its accounting costs. For example, if the owners could have earned a return of 10 per cent elsewhere, the opportunity cost of their funds is 10 per cent times the money they put up. If, after deducting this cost, the business still makes a profit, economists call this 'supernormal profit'.

Supernormal profit

> *Supernormal profit* is the profit over and above the return which the owners could have earned by lending their money elsewhere at the market rate of interest.

Supernormal profits provide the true economic indicator of how well the owners are doing by tying up their funds in the business. Supernormal profits, not accounting profits, are the measure that will explain the incentive to shift resources into or out of a business.

6   These are the two most important adjustments between accounting and economic notions of costs and profits. In other cases there may be minor differences – for example, since it is hard to calculate the resale value of a second-hand factory, economic and accounting approaches to depreciation may vary slightly. In many cases the two approaches are the same – for example, the wages paid by farmers to students for help in picking crops are not only an accounting cost but an economic cost. Without making these payments, farmers would not have been able to attract temporary student labour resources to the activity of crop picking.

The two adjustments between accounting and economic notions of costs and profits

7   Figure 6-4 summarizes the two most important adjustments that must be made to accounting costs and profits to get economic measures of costs and profits.

FIGURE 6-4 ACCOUNTING AND OPPORTUNITY COSTS: TWO IMPORTANT ADJUSTMENTS. Economic costs represents the opportunity costs of resources used in production. Accounting costs include most economic costs but are likely to omit costs of the owner's time and the opportunity cost of financial capital used in the firm. Economic (supernormal) profit deducts the right measure of economic costs from revenues.

ACCOUNTING: INCOME STATEMENT

Revenues	£80 000
Costs	50 000
Accounting profit	£30 000

OPPORTUNITY COSTS: INCOME STATEMENT

Revenues		£80 000
Costs:		
Accounting costs	£50 000	
Cost of owner's time	25 000	
Opportunity cost of financial capital (£30 000) used in firm, at 10%	3 000	78 000
Economic profit (supernormal)		£ 2 000

G. Check your understanding

1. Read the text through again and make notes on the following:

– what is meant by 'retained profits'
– how retained profits affect the balance sheet
– the different interests of accountants and economists
– in what ways, according to the writer, accounting methods are misleading
– what is meant by opportunity cost
– what is meant by supernormal cost
– what the two important adjustments are

2. When you have done that either write a summary of the text or give an oral summary of it.

H. Understanding discourse

A student is not feeling well and has gone to the medical centre. Note down what is wrong with the student and what the doctor tells him to do.

_____

_____

_____

_____

_____

_____

A. Understanding a printed text (1)

The following text discusses in more detail the subject of **macroeconomics**. Look at the way it is divided into sections and paragraphs. Pay attention to the notes in the margin.

Now look at these questions:

1. Look at the first heading and say what you expect to find in the first section.
2. What does the writer distinguish between in the first section?

3. Does he say that one kind of economics is more valuable than the other?
4. What are the main issues introduced in the second section?
5. What organisation is mentioned as playing a role in policy?

Now read the passage through and find the answers to those questions. Remember, you do not have to understand every word to answer them.

THE OVERALL PICTURE

1 *Macroeconomics* is the study of the economy as a whole.
Macroeconomics is concerned not with the details – the price of cigarettes relative to the price of bread, or the output of cars relative to the output of steel – but with the overall picture. In Part 4 we shall study issues such as the determination of the total output of the economy, the aggregate level of unemployment, and the rate of inflation or growth of prices of goods and services as a whole.

2 The distinction between microeconomics and macroeconomics is more

What macroeconomics is

than the difference between economics in the small and economics in the large, which the Greek prefixes *micro* and *macro* suggest. The purpose of the analysis is also different.

3 A model is a deliberate simplification to enable us to pick out the key elements of a problem and think about them clearly. Although we could study the whole economy by piecing together our microeconomic analysis of each and every market, the resulting model would be so cumbersome that it would be hard to keep track of all the economic forces at work. Microeconomics and macroeconomics take different approaches to keep the analysis manageable.

4 Microeconomics places the emphasis on a detailed understanding of particular markets. To achieve this amount of detail or magnification, many of the interactions with other markets are suppressed. In saying that a tax on cars reduces the equilibrium quantity of cars we ignore the question of what the government does with the tax revenue. If the government has to borrow less money, it is possible that interest rates and the exchange rate will fall and that improved inter-

The limitations of models

The different approaches taken

national competitiveness of UK car producers will actually increase the equilibrium output of cars in the UK.

5 Microeconomics is a bit like looking at a horse race through a pair of binoculars. It is great for details, but sometimes we get a clearer picture of the whole race by using the naked eye. Because macroeconomics is concerned primarily with the interaction of different parts of the economy, it relies on a different simplification to keep the analysis manageable. Macroeconomics simplifies the building blocks in order to focus on how they fit together and influence one another.

▼

6   Macroeconomics is concerned with broad aggregates such as the total demand for goods by households or the total spending on machinery and buildings by firms. As in watching the horse race through the naked eye, our notion of the individual details is more blurred but we can give our full attention to the whole picture. We are more likely to notice the horse sneaking up on the rails.

19-1 THE ISSUES

7 We now introduce some of the main issues in macroeconomics. We pose a series of questions which form the theme of the analysis in Part 4.

The inflation rate

8 Inflation   The annual *inflation rate* is the percentage increase per annum in the average price of goods and services. In Chapter 2 we introduced the retail price index (RPI), a weighted average of the prices households pay for goods and services. The percentage annual growth in the RPI is the most commonly used measure of inflation in the UK.

9   What causes inflation? The money supply? Trade Unions? Why do people mind so much about inflation? Does inflation cause unemployment? These are among the questions we shall seek to answer.

Unemployment

10 Unemployment   Unemployment is a measure of the number of people registered as looking for work but without a job. The *unemployment rate* is the percentage of the labour force that is unemployed. The *labour force* is the number of people working or looking for work. It excludes all those, from rich landowners to heroin addicts, who are neither working nor looking for work.

11   Unemployment is now high. Why has it increased so much in the 1980s? Are workers pricing themselves out of jobs by greedy wage claims? Is high unemployment necessary to keep inflation under control, or could the government create more jobs?

Output and growth

12 Output and Growth   Real gross national product (real GNP) measures the total income of the economy. It tells us the quantity of goods and services the economy as a whole can afford to purchase. It is closely related to the total output of the economy. Increases in real GNP are called *economic growth*.

13   What determines the level of real GNP? Does unemployment mean that real GNP is lower than it might be? Why do some countries grow faster than others?

Macroeconomic policy

14 Macroeconomic Policy   Almost every day the newspapers and television refer to the problems of inflation, unemployment, and slow growth. These issues are widely discussed; they help determine the outcome of elections, and make some people interested in learning more about macroeconomics.

15   The government has a variety of policy measures through which it can try to affect the performance of the economy as a whole. It levies taxes,

commissions spending, influences the money supply, interest rates, and the exchange rate, and it sets targets for the output and prices of nationalized industries.

16   What the government can and should do is the subject of lively debate both within the field of economics and in the country at large. As usual, it is important to distinguish between positive issues relating to how the economy works and normative issues relating to priorities or value judgements. In the ensuing chapters we try to make clear which aspects of the policy debate refer to differing beliefs about how the economy works and which aspects refer to differences in priorities or value judgements.

B. Check your understanding

Now read the text carefully, looking up any new items in a dictionary or reference book. Then answer the following questions:

1. What does macroeconomics study?

2. Why is a model not a suitable tool in macroeconomics?

3. What does microeconomics emphasise?

4. What example does the writer use to illustrate the difference between microeconomics and macroeconomics?

5. What do economists most often use to measure inflation?

6. Who are excluded from the unemployment rate and the labour force?

7. Name one possible cause for high unemployment in the 1980s.

8. How is GNP used?

9. How can a government use the exchange rate?

10. What distinction does the writer say is important when debating what the government should do?

C. Increase your vocabulary

1. Look at the first paragraph again. Can you explain the following:
- output
- overall picture
- aggregate level
- inflation

2. Look at paragraph 2 again. The writer points to two prefixes, *micro* and *macro*. Can you think of other words starting with *micro-* and *macro-*?
Or with *hyper-*; *multi-*; *mono-*.

3. Look at paragraph 3 again. What words have the opposite meaning to:
- simple, easy to work with
- by accident or chance
- of no importance
- taking apart

4. Look at paragraph 4 again. What words have the opposite meaning to:
- brought into the open
- not reached or accomplished
- lend

5. Look at paragraph 5 again. Can you explain the following:
- binoculars
- naked eye
- focus

6. Look at paragraph 6 again. What words have the same meaning as:
- idea
- not clearly seen
- total amounts brought together

7. Look at paragraphs 7, 8 and 9 again. What words have the same meaning as:
- be the reason for
- ask
- care

8. Look at paragraphs 10 and 11 again. What words have the opposite meaning to:
- undemanding, moderate
- includes
- destroy

9. Look at paragraphs 12 and 13 again. Can you explain the following:
- GNP
- economic growth

10. Look at paragraphs 14, 15 and 16 again. What words have approximately the same meaning as:
- result
- animated
- gives authority (for something to be done)
- discussion

11. Choose the word that collocates best with the word in *italics*. Remember, the other words may not be 'wrong', just not as natural.
- All governments
raise a wide variety of *taxes*.	☐
levy	☐
collect	☐
- Our government has taken a number of
new *policy* steps	☐
plans	☐
measures	☐
- We expect some
growth in the *economy* this year.	☐
increase	☐
rise	☐
- A model is
an intended *simplification*.	☐
a purposeful	☐
a deliberate	☐
- We expect the *exchange rate* to
decrease over the coming months.	☐
fall	☐
descend	☐
- Macroeconomics is concerned with
wide *aggregates*.	☐
unlimited	☐
broad	☐

D. Check your grammar

Which of the following adjectives can you make the opposite of by using *in-*, *im-*, *ir-*, *dis-* or *un-*.

- affordable
- proportionate
- convenient
- available
- possible
- useful
- frequent
- similar
- plausible
- responsive
- economic
- definite
- relevant
- perceptible
- elastic
- reversible
- wide
- permanent
- responsible
- agreeable

E. Understanding a lecture

You are now going to hear part of a lecture, divided into short sections to help you understand it. As you listen, answer the questions below.

Section 1
- Note down what the lecturer is going to talk about in particular.

- Is this statement correct or incorrect?
  The complete economy consists only of firms and households. ☐
- The lecturer mentions 'economic units'. What do these decide?

Section 2
- Note down what the lecturer intends to ignore.

TABLE 19-5

TRANSACTIONS BY HOUSEHOLDS AND FIRMS

HOUSEHOLDS	FIRMS
Own factors of production which they supply to firms	Use factors of production supplied by households to produce goods and services
Receive incomes from firms in exchange for supplying factors of production	Pay households for use of factors of production
Spend on goods and services produced by firms	Sell goods and services to households

Section 3
- Note down what each row in the table shows.

Section 4
- Label the figure according to the lecturer's instructions.

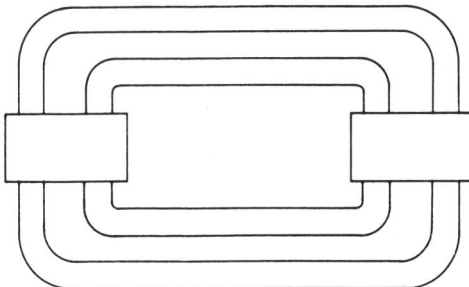

- Note down the three measurements the lecturer lists.

_____

_____

_____

_____

Section 6

- Is this statement correct or incorrect?
  You will get a different estimate depending on the measurement you use. ☐

Section 7

- Is this statement correct or incorrect?
  You will reach a different conclusion if you take into account the questions the lecturer raises. ☐
- Note down the term the lecturer uses to describe this system.

_____

- Note down the three macroeconomic issues the lecturer mentions.

_____

2. Now wind the cassette back to the beginning of the lecture and listen to it again. This time, instead of answering questions, take notes. When you have listened to the whole of the lecture, you will be asked to give an oral summary of it. So make sure you note down the important points.

3. You should also write a summary of the lecture, based on your notes.

F. Understanding a printed text (2)

Read the following text carefully, looking up anything you do not understand.

> **19-4 NATIONAL INCOME ACCOUNTING**
>
> **Measuring GDP**
>
> 1   *Gross domestic product* (GDP) measures the output produced by factors of production located in the domestic economy regardless of who owns these factors.
>
> GDP measures the value of output produced within the economy. Most of this output will be produced by domestic factors of production but there are some exceptions. Suppose Datsun or Peugeot builds a car factory in the UK. They employ UK workers and use machines made in the UK. Their output is part of GDP for the UK. However, the company's profits are owned by shareholders in Japan or France. Hence the value of the factory's output cannot be expected to be the same as the value of incomes earned by UK

What GDP measures

households. Initially we shall simply suppose that we are discussing a country with no links with the rest of the world. Shortly, we shall introduce the rest of the world and show that it is precisely the issue of how to treat payments of profits and other income to foreigners that explains why we have to distinguish GDP from the concept of GNP, which we introduced earlier. When an economy has no transactions with the rest of the world we say that it is a *closed economy*.

What a closed economy is

2   We begin by considering how our simple circular flow diagram should be extended to recognize that transactions do not take place exclusively between a single firm and a single household. Firms hire labour services from households, but they buy raw materials and machinery from other firms. If we include the value of the output of cars in GDP we do not want also to include the value of the steel sold to the car producer which is already in the value of the car.

3   To avoid double counting, we use the concept of value added.

The concept of value added

> *Value added* is the increase in the value of goods as a result of the production process.

Value added is calculated by deducting from the value of the firm's output the cost of the input goods that were used up in the act of producing that output.

4   Closely related to the concept of value added is the distinction between final goods and intermediate goods.

> *Final goods* are goods purchased by the ultimate user. They are either consumer goods purchased by households or capital goods such as machinery which are purchased by firms. *Intermediate goods* are partly finished goods which form inputs to another firm's production process and are used up in that process.

Final goods

Intermediate goods

Thus, ice cream is a final good but steel is an intermediate good which some other firm uses as an input to its production process. In classifying capital goods as final goods we suppose they are not used up in subsequent production. In the language of Chapter 6, we suppose that they do not depreciate or wear out. Shortly, we shall see how depreciation may be handled within this framework.

5   The following example should help you sort out these concepts and it is important that you should study it until you have mastered these ideas. We assume that there are four firms in the economy: a steel producer, a producer of capital goods (machines) used in the car industry, a tyre producer, and a car producer who sells cars to the final consumers, the households. Table 19-6 shows how we may calculate GDP for this simple economy.

An example to help you

6   The steel producer makes £4000 worth of steel, one-quarter of which is sold as an intermediate good to the firm that makes machines and three-quarters of which is sold to the car producer to make cars. If the steel producer also mines the iron ore from which the steel is produced, then

(1)	(2)	(3)	(4)	(5)	(6)	(7)
					EXPENDITURE	
			TRANSACTION	VALUE	ON FINAL	FACTOR
GOOD	SELLER	BUYER	VALUE	ADDED	GOODS	EARNINGS
Steel	Steel producer	Machine producer	£1000	£1000	–	£1000
Steel	Steel producer	Car producer	£3000	£3000	–	£3000
Machine	Machine producer	Car producer	£2000	£1000	£2000	£1000
Tyres	Tyre producer	Car producer	£500	£500	–	£500
Cars	Car producer	Consumers	£5000	£1500	£5000	£1500
Total value of transactions			£11,500			
Gross domestic product (GDP)				£7000	£7000	£7000

TABLE 19-6 CALCULATING GDP

the entire £4000 is value added or net output by the steel firm. This revenue is directly paid out in wages and rents or is residual profits which also accrue to households as income. Hence the first two rows of the last column also add up to £4000. Although firms have spent £4000 buying this steel output, this does not show up as expenditure on final goods since steel is entirely an intermediate good which will be used up in later stages of the production process.

7   The machine manufacturer spends £1000 buying steel input which is then converted into a machine to be sold to the car producer for £2000. The value added of the machine manufacturer is £2000 less the £1000 spent on steel inputs. And this net revenue of £1000 accrues directly or indirectly to households as income or profit. Since the car firm intends to keep the machine, its full value of £2000 is shown under 'Final expenditure'.

8   Like the steel producer, the tyre manufacturer produces an intermediate output which does not show up under final expenditure. If the tyre manufacturer also owns the rubber trees from which the tyres were made, the entire output of £500 is value added and will contribute directly or indirectly to household incomes. If the tyre company bought rubber from a domestic rubber producer we should have to subtract the input value of rubber from the tyre manufacturer's output to obtain value added or net output, but we should have to add another row showing the value added of the company producing the rubber for sale to the tyre company.

9   The car producer spends £3000 on steel and £500 on tyres. Since both are used up during the period in which cars are made, we subtract £3500 from the car output of £5000 to obtain the value added of the car producer. This net revenue pays households for factor services supplied, or is paid to them as profits.

10   Finally, the car producer sells the car for £5000 to the final consumer-households. Only now does the car become a final good and its full price of £5000 is entered as final expenditure.

11   Table 19-6 shows that the gross value of all the transactions that occurred is £11 500, but this overstates the value of the goods the economy has actually produced. For example, the £3000 that the steel producer earned by selling steel to the

car producer is already included in the final value of car output. It is simply double-counting to count this £3000 twice.

12   Column (5) shows the value added at each stage in the production process. In total this comes to £7000, and this is the correct measure of the net output of the economy. Since each producer pays out the corresponding net revenue to households either as direct factor payments or indirectly as profits, household earnings also equal £7000 in the last column of the table. If we simply counted up the payments made to households as income and profits we would get the same measure of the economy's output or GDP.

13   Table 19-6 confirms that we also get the same answer if we measure spending on *final* goods and services. In this case the final users are the households buying the cars and the car producer buying the (everlasting) machinery used to make cars.

What the table confirms

G. Check your understanding

1. Read the text through again and make notes on the following:

– what GDP is
– what GDP measures
– the concept of value added
– final goods
– intermediate goods
– what Table 19-6 shows
– the conclusion the writer comes to

2. When you have done that either write a summary of the text or give an oral summary of it.

H. Understanding discourse

Listen to a tutor giving some advice to a student shortly before his examinations. As you listen, note down the advice the tutor gives.

_____

_____

_____

_____

_____

_____

▼

MONEY AND BANKING

A. Understanding a printed text (1)

The following text will introduce you to the topic of **money**. Look at the way it is divided into sections and paragraphs. Pay attention to the headings and notes in the margin.

Now look at these questions:

1. Look at the main heading and say what you expect the text to be about.
2. Summarise the first function of money.
3. Summarise the second and third functions of money.
4. Summarise the fourth function of money.
5. How many different kinds of money are there?

Now read the passage through and find the answers to those questions. Remember, you do not have to understand every word to answer them.

22-1 MONEY AND ITS FUNCTIONS

The functions of money

1 Although the crucial feature of money is its acceptance as the means of payment or medium of exchange, money has three other functions. It serves as a unit of account, as a store of value, and as a standard of deferred payment. We discuss each of the four functions of money in turn.

The Medium of Exchange

2 Money, the medium of exchange, is used in one-half of almost all exchange. Workers exchange labour services for money. People buy or sell goods in exchange for money. We accept money not to consume it directly but because it can subsequently be used to buy things we do wish to consume. Money is the medium through which people exchange goods and services.

3 To see that society benefits from a medium of exchange, imagine a barter economy.

Barter economies

> A *barter economy* has no medium of exchange. Goods are traded directly or swapped for other goods.

In a barter economy, the seller and the buyer *each* must want something the other has to offer. Each person is simultaneously a seller and a buyer. In order to see a film, you must hand over in exchange a good or service that the cinema manager wants. There has to be a *double coincidence of wants*. You have to find a cinema where the manager wants what you have to offer in exchange.

The disadvantages of a barter economy

4 Trading is very expensive in a barter economy. People must spend a lot of time and effort finding others with whom they can make mutually satisfactory swaps. Since time and effort are scarce resources, a barter economy is wasteful. The use of money – any commodity *generally* accepted in payment for goods, services, and debts – makes the trading process simpler and more efficient.

Other Functions of Money

The unit of account

5 The *unit of account* is the unit in which prices are quoted and accounts are kept.

In Britain prices are quoted in pounds sterling; in France, in French francs. It is usually convenient to use the units in which the medium of exchange is measured as the unit of account as well. However there are exceptions. During the rapid German inflation of 1922–23 when prices in marks were changing very quickly, German shopkeepers found it more convenient to use dollars as the unit of account. Prices were quoted in dollars even though payment was made in marks, the German medium of exchange.

6   Money is a *store of value* because it can be used to make purchases in the future.

Money is a store of value

To be accepted in exchange, money *has* to be a store of value. Nobody would accept money as payment for goods supplied today if the money was going to be worthless when they tried to buy goods with it tomorrow. But money is neither the only nor necessarily the best store of value. Houses, stamp collections, and interest-bearing bank accounts all serve as stores of value. Since money pays no interest and its real purchasing power is eroded by inflation, there are almost certainly better ways to store value.

7   Finally, money serves as a *standard of deferred payment* or a unit of account over time. When you borrow, the amount to be repaid next year is measured in pounds sterling. Although convenient, this is not an essential function of money. UK citizens can get bank loans specifying in dollars the amount that must be repaid next year. Thus the key feature of money is its use as a medium of exchange. For this, it must act as a store of value as well. And it is usually, though not invariably, convenient to make money the unit of account and standard of deferred payment as well.

Money as a standard of deferred payment

8 Different Kinds of Money

In prisoner-of-war camps, cigarettes served as money. In the nineteenth century money was mainly gold and silver coins. These are examples of *commodity money*, ordinary goods with indus-

Commodity money

trial uses (gold) and consumption uses (cigarettes) which also serve as a medium of exchange. To use a commodity money, society must either cut back on other uses of that commodity or devote scarce resources to producing additional quantities of the commodity. But there are less expensive ways for society to produce money.

A *token money* is a means of payment whose value or purchasing power as money greatly exceeds its cost of production or value in uses other than as money.

Token money

A £10 note is worth far more as money than as a 3 × 6 inch piece of high-quality paper. Similarly, the monetary value of most coins exceeds the amount you would get by melting them down and selling off the metals they contain. By collectively agreeing to use token money, society economizes on the scarce resources required to produce money as a medium of exchange. Since the manufacturing costs are tiny, why doesn't everyone make £10 notes?

9 The essential condition for the survival of token money is the restriction of the right to supply it. Private production is illegal.

10 Society enforces the use of token money by making it *legal tender*. The law says it must be accepted as a means of payment.

11 In modern economies, token money is supplemented by IOU money.

An *IOU money* is a medium of exchange based on the debt of a private firm or individual.

A bank deposit is IOU money because it is a debt of the bank. When you have a bank deposit the bank owes you money. You can write a cheque to yourself or a third party and the bank is obliged to pay whenever the cheque is presented. Bank deposits are a medium of exchange because they are generally accepted as payment.

B. Check your understanding

Now read the text carefully, looking up any new items in a dictionary or reference book. Then answer the following questions:

1. Why do people accept money?

2. How are goods exchanged in a barter economy?

3. Why is trading expensive in a barter economy?

4. What is the unit of account in your country?

5. When did Germany not use its own currency?

6. What else does the writer say can be used instead of money as a store of value?

7. What does the writer mean by 'standard of deferred account'?

8. Explain in your own words what 'token money' means.

9. When are people unwilling to accept their own currency?

10. What example of IOU money does the writer give?

C. Increase your vocabulary

1. Look at the first paragraph again. What words have the same meaning as:
● put off till later
● vital

2. Look at paragraphs 2 and 3 again. What words have the opposite meaning to:
● take away
● reject
● planned event

3. Look at paragraph 4 again. What words correspond to these definitions?
● shared by two or more people
● working smoothly and well
● rare

4. Look at paragraph 5 again. Can you explain the following:
● accounts
● medium of exchange
● quoted

5. Look at paragraph 6 again. What words have the same meaning as:
- worn away
- without value

6. Look at paragraph 7 again. What words have the same meaning as:
- always
- giving the name or details of
- serving to avoid difficulty

7. Look at paragraph 8 again. What words have the opposite meaning to:
- in a minor way
- increase
- is less than
- separately
- very large

8. Look at paragraphs 9 and 10 again. What words have the same meaning as:
- against the law
- limitation

9. Look at paragraph 11 again. What words have the opposite meaning to:
- be under no compulsion to
- public

D. Check your grammar

Do you remember?
Some verbs must be followed by the *-ing* form:
He admitted *taking* my book.

Some verbs must be followed by the infinitive:
He agreed *to lend* me his book.

1. Make sentences from the following notes. Think whether you should use the infinitive or the *-ing* form after the verbs:

- he/suggest/read/chapter 5/before/we/go/lecture.

- he/want/spend/more time/study.

- the rain/not stop/fall/until yesterday evening.

- good/manager/try/set/objectives.

- debt/prevent/my country/develop.

- I enjoy/listen/music.

- he/not mind/work/weekends.

- I/not want/risk/fail/my exams.

- he/forget/hand in/essay/last night.

- there/nothing/that shop/worth/buy.

- it/no use/leave/your work/last minute.

- I/miss/watch/college football match/last week.

- he/hope/get/good results/his examinations.

- I/expect/see/increase/interest rates/next month

2. Make nouns from the following adjectives, using *-ness* or *(a/i)bility*:

- complete
- useful
- profitable
- suitable

- comparable
- worthless
- ordinary
- responsible

- indebted
- competitive

E. Understanding a lecture

You are now going to hear part of a lecture, divided into short sections to help you understand it. As you listen, answer the questions below.

Section 1
- What topic is the lecturer going to introduce?

_____

- What is the point of the story?

_____

- Who were the original bankers?

_____

Section 2
- Note down the first development.

_____

- What is the modern word for the 'letter' the lecturer talks about?

_____

- Note down the second development.

_____

Section 3
Are these statements correct or incorrect?
- The goldsmith did not charge the firm interest. ☐
- The goldsmith expected everyone to want their gold at the same time. ☐

Section 4

TABLE 22-1

GOLDSMITHS AS BANKERS

	ASSETS	LIABILITIES
(1) Old-fashioned goldsmith	Gold £100	Deposits £100
(2) Gold lender	Gold £90 + loan £10	Deposits £100
(3) Deposit lender: Step 1	Gold £100 + loan £10	Deposits £110
(4) Step 2	Gold £90 + loan £10	Deposits £100

- Is this statement correct or incorrect?
  Once the goldsmith had made his loan, his liabilities were greater than his assets. ☐

Section 5
- What would we call a deposit today?

_____

- Is this statement correct or incorrect?
  Whether the loan was in gold or as a deposit made no different to the goldsmith. ☐

- Note down what the lecturer means by 'reserves'.

_____

- What is the goldsmith's reserve ratio after making the loan?

_____

Section 7

- The lecturer says people rushed to the goldsmith to get their gold. What term does he use to describe this rush?

_____

- What is the result of a financial panic?

_____

- Note down the question the lecturer gives you, think about it, and then discuss your answer with your colleagues.

_____

2. Now wind the cassette back to the beginning of the lecture and listen to it again. This time, instead of answering questions, take notes. When you have listened to the whole of the lecture, you will be asked to give an oral summary of it. So make sure you note down the important points.

3. You should also write a summary of the lecture, based on your notes.

F. Understanding a printed text (2)

Read the following text carefully, looking up anything you do not understand.

22-3 MODERN BANKING

1 The goldsmith bankers were an early example of a financial intermediary.

> A *financial intermediary* is an institution that specializes in bringing lenders and borrowers together.

A *commercial bank* borrows money from the public, crediting them with a deposit. The deposit is a liability of the bank. It is money owed to depositors. In turn the bank lends money to firms, households, or governments wishing to borrow.

2 Banks are not the only financial intermediaries. Insurance companies, pension funds, and building societies also take in money in order to relend it. The crucial feature of banks is that some of their liabilities are used as a means of payment, and are therefore part of the money stock.

3 *Commercial banks* are financial intermediaries with a government licence to make loans and issue deposits, including deposits against which cheques can be written.

Banks are financial intermediaries

Commercial banks

▼

We begin by looking at the present-day UK banking system. Although the details vary from country to country, the general principle is much the same everywhere.

4   In the UK, the commercial banking system comprises about 600 registered banks, the National Girobank operating through post offices, and about a dozen trustee savings banks. Much the most important single group is the London clearing banks. The clearing banks are so named because they have a central clearing house for handling payments by cheque.

Clearing banks

The clearing system

> A *clearing system* is a set of arrangements in which debts between banks are settled by adding up all the transactions in a given period and paying only the net amounts needed to balance inter-bank accounts.

How the system works

Suppose you bank with Barclays but visit a supermarket that banks with Lloyds. To pay for your shopping you write a cheque against your deposit at Barclays. The supermarket pays this cheque into its account at Lloyds. In turn, Lloyds presents the cheque to Barclays which will credit Lloyds' account at Barclays and debit your account at Barclays by an equivalent amount. Because you purchased goods from a supermarket using a different bank, a transfer of funds between the two banks is required. Crediting or debiting one bank's account at another bank is the simplest way to achieve this.

5   However on the same day someone else, call her Joan Groover, is probably writing a cheque on a Lloyd's deposit account to pay for some stereo equipment from a shop banking with Barclays. The stereo shop pays the cheque into its Barclays' account, increasing its deposit. Barclays then pay the cheque into its account at Lloyds where Ms Groover's account is simultaneously debited. Now the transfer flows from Lloyds to Barclays.

6   Although in both cases the cheque writer's account is debited and the cheque recipient's account is credited, it does not make sense for the two banks to make two separate inter-bank transactions between themselves. The clearing system calculates the *net* flows between the member clearing banks and these are the settlements that they make between themselves. Thus the system of clearing cheques represents another way society reduces the costs of making transactions.

The Balance Sheet of the London Clearing Banks

The balance sheet of the London clearing banks

7   Table 22-2 shows the balance sheet of the London clearing banks. Although more complex, it is not fundamentally different from the balance sheet of the goldsmith-banker shown in Table 22-1. We begin by discussing the asset side of the balance sheet.

8   Cash assets are notes and coin in the banks' vaults just as the goldsmiths held gold in their vaults. However, modern banks' cash assets also

include their cash reserves deposited with the Bank of England. The Bank of England (usually known as the Bank) is the *central bank* or banker to the commercial banks.

The central bank

9 Apart from cash, the other entries on the asset side of the balance sheet show money that has been lent out or used to purchase interest-earning assets. The second item, bills and market loans, shows short-term lending in liquid assets.

> *Liquidity* refers to the speed and the certainty with which an asset can be converted back into money, whenever the asset-holders desire. Money itself is thus the most liquid asset of all.

Liquidity

10 The third item, advances, shows lending to households and firms. A firm that has borrowed to see it through a sticky period may not be able to repay whenever the bank demands. Thus, although advances represent the major share of clearing bank lending, they are not very liquid forms of bank lending. The fourth item, securities, shows bank purchases of interest-bearing long-term financial assets. These can be government bonds or industrial shares. Although these assets are traded daily on the stock exchange, so in principle these securities can be cashed in any time the bank wishes, their price fluctuates from day to day. Banks cannot be certain how much they will get when they sell out. Hence financial investment in securities is also illiquid.

11 The final two items on the asset side of Table 22-2 show lending in foreign currencies and miscellaneous bank assets whose details need not concern us. Total assets of the London clearing banks in May 1986 were £200.1 billion. We now examine how the equivalent liabilities were made up.

12 Deposits are chiefly of two kinds: sight deposits and time deposits. Whereas sight deposits can be withdrawn on sight whenever the depositor wishes, a minimum period of notification must be given before time deposits can be withdrawn. Sight deposits are the bank accounts against which we write cheques, thereby running down our deposits without giving the bank any prior warning. Whereas most banks do not pay interest on sight deposits or chequing accounts, they can afford to pay interest on time deposits. Since they have notification of any withdrawals, they have plenty of time to sell off some of their high-

Their liabilities

TABLE 22-2
BALANCE SHEET OF LONDON CLEARING BANKS, MAY 1986

ASSETS	£ b	LIABILITIES	£ b
Sterling: Cash	2.9	Sterling: Sight deposits	54.1
Bills and market loans	34.7	Time deposits	59.9
Advances	83.0	CDs (Certificates of deposit)	8.1
Securities	9.4		
Lending in other currencies	54.6	Deposits in other currencies	46.2
Miscellaneous assets	15.5	Miscellaneous liabilities	31.8
TOTAL ASSETS	200.1	TOTAL LIABILITIES	200.1

Source: Bank of England Quarterly Bulletin.

interest investments or call in some of their high-interest loans in order to have the money to pay out depositors.

13 Certificates of deposit (CDs) are an extreme form of time deposit where the bank borrows from the public for a specified time period and knows exactly when the loan must be repaid. The final liability items in Table 22-2 show deposits in foreign currencies and miscellaneous liabilities such as cheques in the process of clearance.

G. Check your understanding

1. Read the text through again and make notes on the following:

- the role of banks
- commercial banks
- the clearing system
- the balance sheet of the London clearing banks
- their assets
- their liabilities

2. When you have done that either write a summary of the text or give an oral summary of it.

H. Understanding discourse

Listen to a tutor giving some students advice about how to use the library to improve their work. Note down the advice.

_____

_____

_____

_____

_____

_____

CENTRAL BANKING

A. Understanding a printed text (1)

The following text will introduce you to the topic of **central banking**. Look at the way it is divided into sections and paragraphs. Pay attention to the headings and notes in the margin.

Now look at these questions:

1. Look at the main heading and say what you expect the text to be about.
2. What does the writer say he is going to examine in this text?

3. What is the second section essentially about?
4. What is the third section essentially about?
5. In the writer's opinion, can a central bank influence the money supply?

Now read the passage through and find the answers to those questions. Remember, you do not have to understand every word to answer them.

23-2 THE BANK AND THE MONEY SUPPLY

1 In this section we study the ways in which a central bank can affect the supply of money in the economy. The narrowest measure M1 of the money supply is currency in circulation outside the banking system plus the sight deposits of commercial banks against which the private sector can write cheques. Thus the money supply is partly a liability of the Bank (currency in private circulation) and partly a liability of commercial banks (chequing accounts of the general public).

M1

2 In the last chapter we introduced the *monetary base*, the currency supplied by the Bank both to the commercial banks and to private circulation, and the *money multiplier*, the extent to which the money supply is a multiple of the monetary base. We saw that the money multiplier was larger the smaller the cash reserve ratio of the commercial banks and the smaller the private sector's desired ratio of cash to bank deposits.

The monetary base

The money multiplier

3 We now describe the three most important instruments through which the Bank *might* seek to affect the money supply: reserve requirements, the discount rate, and open market operations.

Reserve Requirements

4 A *required reserve ratio* is a minimum ratio of cash reserves to deposits that the central bank requires commercial banks to hold.
If a reserve requirement is in force, commercial banks can hold more than the required cash reserves but they cannot hold less. If their cash falls below the required amount, they must immediately borrow cash, usually from the central bank, to restore their required reserve ratio.

Required reserve ratio

5 Suppose the commercial banking system has £1 million in cash and for strictly commercial purposes would normally maintain cash reserves equal to 5 per cent of sight deposits. Since sight deposits will be 20 times cash reserves, the banking system will create £20 million of sight deposits

How a required reserve ratio works

against its £1 million cash reserves. Suppose the Bank now imposes a reserve requirement that banks must hold cash reserves of at least 10 per cent of sight deposits. Now banks can create only £10 million sight deposits against their cash reserves of £1 million.

6   Thus, when the central bank imposes a reserve requirement in excess of the reserve ratio that prudent banks would anyway have maintained, the effect is to reduce the creation of bank deposits, reduce the value of the money multiplier, and reduce the money supply for any given monetary base. Similarly, when a particular reserve requirement is already in force, any increase in the reserve requirement will reduce the money supply.

The effect on banks

7   When the central bank imposes a reserve requirement in excess of the reserves that banks would otherwise have wished to hold, the banks are creating fewer deposits and undertaking less lending than they would really like. Thus a reserve requirement acts like a tax on banks by forcing them to hold a higher fraction of their total assets as bank reserves and a lower fraction as loans earning high interest rates. Can the banks do anything about it?

8   Although there are profitable lending opportunities, the banks can take advantage of them only if they can increase their cash reserves. In principle, they could try to borrow cash from the central bank. If the point of a reserve requirement is to reduce the money supply, the central bank will be reluctant to lend banks the cash they want to make additional loans, increase deposits, and expand the money supply. With lucrative lending opportunities around, the banks may be able to induce the private sector to exchange cash in circulation for bank deposits. Banks can offer more generous interest rates on time deposits or stay open later to encourage people to make greater use of chequing facilities. By attracting more cash from the general public, banks may then be able to restore former levels of deposit lending, though there is then the danger that the central bank will raise the reserve requirement still higher.

Special deposits

9   One form of reserve requirement that has been especially popular in the UK is the use of *special deposits*. Commercial banks were required to deposit some of their cash reserves in a special deposit at the Bank, and this money could *not* be counted as part of the banks' cash reserves in meeting their reserve requirements. Varying the amount required as special deposits gave the Bank another lever for controlling deposit creation by the banking system and the size of the money multiplier.

The Discount Rate

10 The second instrument of monetary control available to the central bank is the discount rate.

The discount rate

> The *discount rate* is the interest rate that the Bank charges when the commercial banks want to borrow money.

When the discount rate was an important part of monetary control in the UK it used to be known as the Bank Rate, or Minimum Lending Rate (MLR).

11   Suppose banks think the *minimum* safe ratio of cash to deposits is 10 per cent. For the purposes of this argument it does not matter whether this figure is a commercial judgement or a required ratio imposed by the Bank. On any particular day, banks are likely to have a bit of cash in hand. Say their cash reserves are 12 per cent of deposits. How far dare they let their cash reserves fall towards the minimum level of 10 per cent?

12   Banks have to balance the interest rate they will get on extra lending with the dangers and costs involved if there is a sudden flood of withdrawals which push their cash reserves below the critical 10 per cent figure. This is where the discount rate comes in. Suppose market interest rates are 8 per cent and the central bank makes it known it is prepared to lend to commercial banks at 8 per cent. Commercial banks may as well lend up to the hilt and drive their cash reserves down to the minimum 10 per cent of deposits. The banks are lending at 8 per cent and, if the worst comes to the worst and they are short of cash, they can always borrow from the Bank at 8 per cent. Banks cannot lose by lending as much as possible.

13   Suppose however that the Bank announces that, although market interest rates are 8 per cent, it will lend to commercial banks only at the penalty rate of 10 per cent. Now a bank with cash reserves of 12 per cent may conclude that it is not worth making the extra loans at 8 per cent interest that would drive its cash reserves down to the minimum of 10 per cent of deposits. There is too high a risk that sudden withdrawals will then force the bank to borrow from the Bank at 10 per cent interest. It will have lost money by making these extra loans. It makes more sense to hold some excess cash reserves against the possibility of a sudden withdrawal.

14   Thus, by setting the discount rate at a penalty level in excess of the general level of interest rates, the Bank can induce commercial banks voluntarily to hold additional cash reserves. Since bank deposits now become a lower multiple of banks' cash reserves, the money multiplier is reduced and the money supply is lower for any given level of the monetary base.

What banks have to balance

When it is not worth banks lending all they can

The power of the Bank

B. Check your understanding

Now read the text carefully, looking up any new items in a dictionary or reference book. Then answer the following questions:

1. Whose liability is M1?

2. What is the monetary base?

▼

3. Explain in your own words what a 'required reserve ratio' is.

4. What is the effect of the Bank imposing a reserve requirement?

5. Why does a reserve requirement act like a tax on banks?

6. What can banks do about this 'tax'?

7. Explain in your own words what a 'special deposit' is.

8. What is another term for Bank Rate or MLR?

9. Why can banks not lose by lending as much as possible?

10. Under what circumstances is it not worth banks lending as much as possible?

C. Increase your vocabulary

1. Look at the first paragraph again. Using your dictionary, find a word or words that have the same meaning as:
- central
- narrowest
- partly

2. Look at paragraphs 2 and 3 again. Can you explain in your own words:
- monetary base
- money multiplier
- cash reserve ratio
- instruments

3. Look at paragraphs 4 and 5 again. What words correspond to these definitions?
- make normal again; bring back (to a former condition)
- keep in good order
- precisely (limited)

4. Look at paragraph 6 again. What words have the opposite meaning to:
- in a different way
- not binding
- careless

5. Look at paragraph 7 again. What words have the same meaning as:
- wanting
- compelling

6. Look at paragraph 8 again. What words have the same meaning as:
- profitable
- reason for
- make larger
- giving, ready to give

7. Look at paragraph 9 again. Can you explain the following:
- cash reserves
- reserve requirements

8. Look at paragraphs 10 and 11 again. Using your dictionary, find a word or words that have the same meaning as:
- charges
- argument
- commercial

9. Look at paragraph 12 again. Can you explain the following:
- sudden flood of withdrawals
- up to the hilt
- if the worst comes to the worst

10. Look at paragraph 13 again. What words have the same meaning as:
- is more sensible
- push down
- in case of

11. Look at paragraph 14 again. What words have the opposite meaning to:
- compulsorily
- unknown

D. Check your grammar

ASKING QUESTIONS AND TAKING NOTES

Can you ask questions in a way that makes sure you get the information you want? And that you understand the answers? You have to write a short summary on Open Market Operations. You must say what an Open Market Operation is, and how it affects the monetary base. The teacher has the information you need to do this. Ask for the information you need and note down the answers. Then write a short summary.

_____

_____

_____

_____

_____

_____

_____

_____

E. Understanding a lecture

You will now hear part of a lecture, divided into short sections to help you understand it. As you listen, answer the questions below.

Section 1
* What is the lecturer going to talk about?

_____

* The lecturer names three scarce resources. What are they?

_____

Section 2
* Note down what can cause a financial panic.

_____

* Is this statement correct or incorrect?
  A central bank can reduce the risk of a financial panic by providing cash.   ☐

Section 3
* Note down the term the lecturer gives you.

_____

* What is the effect of this role?

_____

▼

● Note down the second main function.

_____

● What does PSBR stand for?

_____

_____

Section 5————————————————————————————————————

● Note down the first way in which the government can finance the PSBR.

_____

_____

Section 6————————————————————————————————————

● Note down the second way in which the government can finance the PSBR.

_____

_____

2. Now wind the cassette back to the beginning of the lecture and listen to it again. This time, instead of answering questions, take notes. When you have listened to the whole of the lecture, you will be asked to give an oral summary of it. So make sure you note down the important points.

3. You should also write a summary of the lecture, based on your notes.

F. Understanding a printed text (2)

Read the following text carefully, looking up anything you do not understand.

23-4 THE DEMAND FOR MONEY

1 In 1965 the amount of money (M1) in the UK was £7.6 billion. By 1985 it was £65 billion. Why were UK residents prepared to hold nine times as much money in 1985 as in 1965? Answering that question will introduce us to the factors that determine money demand, which in turn sets the stage for understanding how monetary policy affects the economy.

The three key variables

2   We single out three key variables that determine money demand: interest rates, the price level or average price of goods and services, and real income. Before examining whether movements in these variables can explain the ninefold increase in money holdings between 1965 and 1985, we reconsider why people hold money at all.

The Motives for Holding Money

3 Money is a stock. It is the quantity of circulating currency and bank deposits *held* at any given time. Holding money is not the same as *spending* money when we buy a meal or go to the cinema. We hold money now in order to spend it later.

Money is a medium of exchange

4   The distinguishing feature of money is its use as a medium of exchange, for which it must also serve as a store of value. It is in these two functions of money that we must seek the reasons why people wish to hold it.

▼

5 People can hold their wealth in various forms – money, bills, bonds, equities, and property. For simplicity we assume that there are only two assets: money, the medium of exchange that pays no interest, and bonds, which we use to stand for all other interest-bearing assets that are not directly a means of payment. As people earn income, they add to their wealth. As they spend, they deplete their wealth. How should people divide their wealth at any instant between money and bonds?

6 There is an obvious cost in holding any money at all.

> The opportunity cost of holding money is the interest given up by holding money rather than bonds.

People will hold money only if there is a benefit to offset this cost. We now consider what that benefit might be.

7 The Transactions Motive In a monetary economy we use money to purchase goods and services and receive money in exchange for the goods and services we sell. Without money, making transactions by direct barter would be costly in time and effort. Holding money economizes on the time and effort involved in undertaking transactions.

8 If all transactions were perfectly synchronized, we would earn revenue from sales of goods and income from sales of factor services at the same instant we made purchases of the goods and services we wish to consume. Except at that instant, we need hold no money at all.

> The *transactions motive* for holding money reflects the fact that payments and receipts are not perfectly synchronized.

We need to hold money between receiving payments and making subsequent purchases.

9 How much money we need to hold depends on two things, the value of the transactions we wish to make and the degree of synchronization of our payments and receipts. Money is a nominal variable not a real variable. We do not know how much £100 will buy until we know the price of goods. If all prices double, both our receipts and our payments will double in nominal terms. To make the same transactions as before we will need to hold twice as much money. Putting this differently:

> The demand for money is a demand for *real* money balances.

We need a given amount of real money, nominal money deflated by the price level, to undertake a given quantity of total transactions. Hence when the price level doubles, other things equal we expect the demand for nominal money balances to double, leaving the demand for real money balances unaltered. People want money because of its purchasing power in terms of the goods it will buy.

10 The second factor affecting the transactions motive for holding money is the degree of synchronization of payments and receipts. Suppose that, instead of spreading their shopping evenly throughout the week, households do all their shopping on the day they get a salary cheque

▼

from their employers. Over the week, national income and total transactions are unaltered, but people now *hold* less money over the week.

11 A nation's habits for making payments change only slowly. In our simplified model we assume that the degree of synchronization remains constant over time. Thus we focus on real national income as *the* measure of the transactions motive for holding *real* money balances.

12 The Precautionary Motive Thus far we have assumed that people know exactly when they will obtain receipts and make payments. But of course we live in an uncertain world. This uncertainty about the precise timing of receipts and payments gives rise to a precautionary motive for holding money.

13 Suppose you decide to buy a lot of interest-earning bonds and try to get by with only a small amount of money holdings. You are walking down the street and spot a great bargain in a shop window. But you do not have enough money to take advantage immediately of this opportunity. By the time you have arranged for some of your interest-earning bonds to be sold off in exchange for money, the sale may be over. Someone else may have snapped up the video recorder on sale at half price. This is the precautionary motive for holding money.

> In an uncertain world, there is a *precautionary motive* to hold money. In advance, we decide to hold money to meet contingencies the exact nature of which we cannot yet foresee.

If we had foreseen the contingency we would have had plenty of time to cash in interest-earning bonds to have money available. If we did not have to take advantage of the transactions opportunity immediately, it would not matter that it was unforeseen: we could still cash in our bonds at our leisure and buy the half-price video recorder. We forgo interest and carry money for precautionary reasons, because having ready money allows us to snap up unforeseen bargains, or stave off unforeseen crises by making immediate payments.

14 Together, the transactions and precautionary motives provide the main reasons for holding the medium of exchange. They are the motives most relevant to the benefits from holding the narrow definition of money M1.

15 The Asset Motive Suppose we forget all about the need to transact. We think of a wealthy individual or a firm deciding in which assets to hold wealth. At some distant date there may be a prospect of finally spending some of that wealth, but in the short run the objective is to earn a good rate of return.

16 Some assets, such as industrial shares, on average pay a high rate of return but are also quite risky. Some years their return is *very* high but in other years it is negative. When share prices fall, shareholders can make a capital loss which swamps any dividend payment to which they are entitled. Other assets are much less risky, but their rate of return tends to be much lower than the average return on risky assets.

17   How should people divide their portfolios of financial investments between safe and risky assets? We discussed this question in detail in Chapter 13 and you might like to reread Sections 13-4 and 13-5. We concluded that, since people dislike risk, they will not put all their eggs in one basket. As well as holding some risky assets, they will keep some of their wealth in safe assets. Although on average this portfolio will earn a lower rate of return, it will help avoid absolute disaster in bad years.

> The *asset motive* for holding money arises because people dislike risk. People are prepared to sacrifice a high average rate of return to obtain a portfolio with a lower but more predictable rate of return.

The asset motive for holding money is important when we consider why people hold broad measures of money such as sterling M3. It is much less relevant when we consider why people hold the medium of exchange as measured by M1. Why? Because if we are going to lend or invest money for any length of time, we can put it in a time deposit, which is safe but earns interest, rather than in a sight deposit or in cash which, though equally safe, earn no interest. Since time deposits are included in sterling M3 but not in M1, the asset motive is of interest chiefly for wider measures of money. However, as more sight deposits start to bear interest, this distinction is breaking down.

People dislike risk

G. Check your understanding

Read through the text again and make notes on the following:
- what determines money demand   – the Transactions Motive
- what money is   – The Precautionary Motive
- how people hold money   – The Asset Motive
When you have done that either write a summary of the text or give an oral summary of it.

H. Understanding discourse

Listen to a tutor giving some students advice about revisions. Note down the advice.

_____

_____

_____

_____

_____

INTERNATIONAL TRADE

A. Understanding a printed text (1)

The following text will introduce you to the topic of **international trade**. Look at the way it is divided into sections and paragraphs. Pay attention to the headings, tables and notes in the margin.

Now look at these questions:

1. From the heading, what do you expect the text to be about?
2. Explain what Table 31-1 shows in your own words.

3. Explain what Table 31-2 shows in your own words.
4. Explain what Table 31-3 shows in your own words.
5. Explain what Table 31-4 shows in your own words.

Now read the passage through and find the answers to those questions. Remember, you do not have to understand every word to answer them.

31-1 THE PATTERN OF WORLD TRADE

How to calculate international trade

1 Since every international transaction has both a buyer and a seller, one country's imports must be another country's exports. To get an idea of how much trade takes place, we can count the total value of exports by all countries or the total value of imports. They must be exactly the same. And to count both imports and exports would be to count every transaction twice.

2 Table 31-1 shows the value of world exports for selected years and, as a benchmark, the level of world trade relative to GNP in the world's largest single economy, the United States.

World trade has expanded

3 Two facts stand out. First, in real terms world trade has expanded very rapidly since 1950, at an average annual rate of 8 per cent. International trade has been playing an increasingly important part in national economies. Between 1960 and 1985, UK exports as a fraction of GNP rose from 20 per cent to nearly 30 per cent. Details for selected countries are shown in Table 31-2. By 1985, world exports were about 18 per cent of world GNP.

TABLE 31-1
THE VALUE OF WORLD EXPORTS

	1928	1935	1950	1973	1980	1985
World exports (billions of 1980 £)	139	58	89	415	881	1054
World exports (% of US GNP)	57	27	20	40	71	65

Sources: League of Nations, Europe's Trade, Geneva, 1941; IMF, International Financial Statistics, National Income Accounts of the United States, 1928–49.

4   Second, the Great Depression of the 1930s and the Second World War virtually destroyed international trade. Taking US GNP as a benchmark, it was not until the mid-1970s that world trade again reached its 1928 ratio to US GNP.

5   As trade has grown, both in absolute terms and relative to the size of national economies, the interdependence of national economies has increased. Like many of the countries shown in Table 31-2, Britain is now a very open economy. Events in other countries affect our daily lives much more than they did 20 years ago. We now look at the facts about who trades with whom.

World Trade Patterns

6 In Table 31-3 we show the pattern of trade among four major groups of countries. The industrial or developed countries include Western Europe, North America, Japan, Australia, and New Zealand, the rich countries with the largest share of world trade and world income. The oil-producing countries such as Saudi Arabia and Kuwait are shown separately. The Soviet bloc comprises Russia and the countries of Eastern Europe. The remaining countries are grouped as the non-oil LDCs. We study these *less developed countries* – ranging from the very poor, such as China and India, to the nearly rich, such as Brazil and Mexico – in greater detail in Chapter 33.

7   The entries in Table 31-3 are the percentage of world exports from countries in the left-hand column to the countries in the first four column heads. Thus, for example, 43.4 per cent of world exports are from industrial countries to other industrial countries.

8   What can we learn from Table 31-3? First, almost half of world trade is between the industrialized countries. Second, these countries

TABLE 31-2

EXPORTS AS A PERCENTAGE OF GNP

	1960	1984
Belgium	39	79
Germany	19	31
UK	21	29
Italy	14	27
Japan	11	15
USA	5	8

Sources: IMF, *International Financial Statistics*; OECD, *Historical Statistics.*

TABLE 31-3 ▪▪▪▪▪▪

WORLD TRADE PATTERNS, 1983
(Percentage of world exports)

	EXPORTS TO*				% SHARE OF	
EXPORTS FROM	INDUSTRIAL COUNTRIES	OIL PRODUCERS	NON-OIL LDCs	SOVIET BLOC	WORLD TRADE	WORLD INCOME
Industrial countries	43.4	5.3	9.2	2.8	63.2	66.7
Oil producers	6.5	0.3	2.9	0.3	10.1	5.8
Non-oil LDCs	9.2	1.0	3.3	0.9	15.7	13.7
Soviet bloc	3.3	0.5	1.6	5.7	11.1	13.9

* Figures in blue show percentage of world trade arising from trade between countries in the same group.
Source: GATT, *International Trade,* 1983/84; World Bank, *World Development Report,* 1985.

have about two-thirds of world exports, world income, and world imports. World trade is very much organized around these countries. The only significant entry in the table that does not involve industrial countries is trade within the Soviet bloc, which trades mostly among its member countries.

The Commodity Composition of World Trade

9 Table 31-4 shows which goods are being internationally traded. It distinguishes between *primary commodities* (agricultural commodities, minerals, and fuels) and manufactured or processed commodities (chemicals, steel, cars, etc.). Note in particular the sharply declining share of *non-fuel* primary commodities, which fell from 39.3 per cent of world trade in 1955 to only 18.5 per cent in 1984.[1] In contrast, the share of manufactures and of fuels in world trade each rose by about 10 per cent during this period. The increase in the value of fuel exports is due mainly to the dramatic rise in real oil prices after 1973.

10 For trade in manufactures, engineering goods have become increasingly significant, as have road vehicles. The increased share of engineering goods is one of the significant trends in world trade to which we return when discussing theories of the gains from international trade.

Primary commodities and manufactured commodities

TABLE 31-4 ▪▪▪▪▪▪

THE COMPOSITION OF WORLD EXPORTS

% share of:	1955	1984
Primary commodities:	50.5	38.3
Food, agricultural goods	22.3	11.0
Fuels	11.2	19.8
Other minerals	3.8	1.8
Manufactures:	49.5	60.0
Road vehicles	3.6	7.5
Engineering goods	21.4	33.9
Textiles and clothing	6.0	5.2

Source: GATT, *International Trade 1984/85; Networks of World Trade 1955–76,* GATT, Geneva.

B. Check your understanding

Now read the text carefully, looking up any new items in a dictionary or reference book. Then answer the following questions:

1. How can international trade be calculated?

2. What is the first fact that Table 31-1 demonstrates?

3. What is the second fact that Table 31-1 demonstrates?

4. What has resulted from the growth of international trade?

5. What is an LDC?

6. Which major group does your country fall into? Can you explain why?

7. Round which countries is most world trade organised?

8. What are tomatoes an example of?

9. What is a computer an example of?

10. What kinds of good have become more important recently?

C. Increase your vocabulary

1. Look at the first paragraph again. What words have the same meaning as:
- precisely
- deal, business arrangement

2. Look at paragraphs 2 and 3 again. What words have the opposite meaning to:
- slowly
- not chosen

3. Look at paragraphs 4 and 5 again. What words have the same meaning as:
- happenings
- as good as

4. Look at paragraphs 6, 7 and 8 again. Using your dictionary, find words that have the same or approximately the same meaning as:
- comprises
- separately
- remaining
- significant
- mostly

5. Look at paragraphs 9 and 10. What words correspond to these definitions:
- sudden or exciting
- comparison so that differences are pointed out
- getting less
- cars, lorries etc.
- increase of possessions or wealth

6. Look at paragraph 11 again. Can you explain the following:
- breakdown
- raw materials
- partly finished manufactures

7. Look at paragraph 12 again. What words have the same meaning as:
- controlled or influenced by
- explain the cause of
- by itself/themselves

8. Look at paragraph 13 again. Can you explain the following:
- textiles
- consumer durables

D. Check your grammar

Make complete sentences out of the following notes, putting the verbs in brackets in the right tense. Then arrange the sentences into a paragraph. Make sure that the sentences follow each other logically and that the paragraph makes sense. Head your paragraph:

GATT (General Agreement on Tariffs and Trade)

1. rounds/steadily/under/of/successive/GATT/tariffs (fall)

2. tariffs/ensuing/half/the/then/by/nearly/in/15 years (reduce)

3. war/the/determination/to see/a/world trade/after collective/there (be; restore)

4. start/throughout/the/world/the/at/probably/low/as/as/they/1980s/of/the/tariff levels (be; be)

5. in 1939/level/about/US/one-fifth/1960/their/by/only/tariffs (be)

6. such/IMF/bodies/as/the/number/GATT/and/countries/of/large/a (set up; sign)

7. this/success/GATT/at/restrictions/partly/from/in/trade/the/least/of (arise; remove)

8. UK/wartime/mid-1950s/quotas/the/in/system/imports/of/the/on/the/by (dismantle)

9. a/to reduce/and/successively/this/trade/tariffs/restrictions/commitment (be; dismantle)

10. decades/rapid/three/trade/of/world/growth (see)

E. Understanding a lecture

You are now going to hear part of a lecture, divided into short sections to help you understand it. As you listen, answer the questions below.

Section 1
- Note down what the lecturer is going to talk about.

- Note down the first fact.

- Note down the second fact.

- Note down the third fact.

Section 2
Are these statements correct or incorrect?
- LDCs have no complaints against industrialised countries. ☐
- LDCs would like to be able to act like oil-producing countries. ☐

- Is this statement correct or incorrect?
  Industrialised countries welcome manufactured goods from LDCs. ☐

Are these statements correct or incorrect?
- There is a trade dispute between Japan and the USA and Europe. ☐
- The lecturer takes sides in this dispute. ☐

2. Now wind the cassette back to the beginning of the lecture and listen to it again. This time, instead of answering questions, take notes. When you have listened to the whole of the lecture, you will be asked to give an oral summary of it. So make sure you note down the important points.

3. You should also write a summary of the lecture, based on your notes.

F. Understanding a printed text (2)

Read the following text carefully, looking up anything you do not understand.

31-6 GOOD AND BAD ARGUMENTS FOR TARIFFS

1 Table 31-11 lists some of these arguments. We group them under several headings. The *first-best* argument is a case where a tariff is *the* best way to achieve a given objective. *Second-best* arguments are cases where the policy would indeed be beneficial but where there is another policy that would be even better if only it could be implemented. If possible we should always use first-best policies, but sometimes we have to make do with second-best ones. Non-arguments are cases in which the claimed benefits are partly or completely fallacious.

First and second-best arguments

TABLE 31-11
ARGUMENTS FOR TARIFFS

FIRST-BEST	SECOND-BEST		STRATEGIC	NON-ARGUMENTS
Foreign trade monopoly	Way of life Anti-luxury Defence	Infant industry Revenue	Games against foreigners	Cheap foreign labour

The Optimal Tariff: The First-best Argument for Tariffs

2 In presenting the case for free trade, we were careful to assume that the domestic economy could import as many cars as it wished without bidding up the world price of cars. For a small

First-best and second-best arguments

▼

economy this may be a reasonable assumption. However, when a country's imports form a significant share of the world market for a commodity, a higher level of imports is likely to bid up the world price of the good being imported.

3   In this case, the world price of the last unit imported is *lower* than the true cost of the last import to the domestic economy. The domestic economy should recognize that, in demanding another unit of imports, it raises the price it has to pay on the quantity already being imported. But in a free trade world without tariffs, each individual will think only about the price that he or she pays. Although no single individual bids up the price, collectively the individuals of the domestic economy bid up the price of imports.

4   Under free trade, each individual buys imports up to the point at which the benefit to that individual equals the world price the individual must pay. Since the collective cost of the last import exceeds its world price, the cost of that import to society exceeds its benefit. There are too many imports. Society will gain by restricting imports until the benefit of the last import equals its cost to society as a whole. When the tariff is set at the level required to achieve this, it is called the *optimal tariff*. Only when a country does not bid up the world price of its imports is the cost to society of the last unit imported equal to the world price. Then and only then is the optimal tariff zero. There is no longer any reason to discourage imports. That is the case for free trade under those circumstances.

Optimal tariffs

5   The optimal tariff is a straightforward application of the principles of efficient resource allocation which we discussed in Part 3. There is another way to see how the optimal tariff works. When a country faces an upward-sloping supply curve for its imports, levying a tariff will reduce the world price of the good by moving foreign suppliers down their supply curve as their output falls. Effectively this is a transfer from foreign suppliers, who lose out, to the importing country, which gains.

Second-best Arguments for Tariffs

6 We now introduce the principle of targeting.
        The *principle of targeting* says that the most efficient way to attain a given objective is to use a policy that influences that activity directly. Policies that attain the objective but

The principle of targeting

▼

152

also influence other activities are second-best because they distort these other activities.

The optimal tariff is a first-best application of the principle of targeting precisely because the source of the problem is a divergence between social and private marginal costs in trade itself. That is why a tariff on trade is the most efficient solution. The arguments for tariffs that we now examine are all second-best arguments because the original source of the problem does not directly lie in trade. And the principle of targeting assures us that there are ways to solve these problems at a lower net social cost, without having to incur the deadweight burden or waste triangles such as those shown in Figure 31-4.

7 Way of Life   Suppose society wishes to preserve inefficient farmers or craft industries. It believes that the old way of life, or sense of community, should be preserved. Therefore it levies tariffs to protect such groups from foreign competition.

8   But there is a cheaper way to attain this objective. A tariff helps domestic producers but also hurts domestic consumers through higher prices. A production subsidy would still keep farmers in business and, by tackling the problem directly, would avoid hurting consumers.

9 Suppressing luxuries   Some poor countries believe it is wrong to allow their few rich citizens to buy Rolls Royces or luxury yachts when society needs its resources to stop people starving. A tariff on imports of luxuries will reduce their consumption but, by raising the domestic price, may also provide an incentive for domestic producers to use scarce resources to produce them. A consumption tax tackles the problem directly, and is a more efficient tool.

10 Defence   Some countries believe that, in case there is a war, it is important to preserve domestic industries that produce food or jet fighters. Again, a production subsidy rather than an import tariff is the most efficient way to meet this objective.

11 Infant Industries   One of the most common arguments for a tariff is that a tariff is needed to allow infant industries to get started. Suppose there is *learning by doing*. Only by actually being

Way of life

Luxuries

Defence

Infant industries

in business will firms learn how to reduce costs and become as efficient as foreign competitors. A tariff is needed to provide protection to new or infant industries until they have mastered the business and can compete on equal terms with more experienced foreign suppliers.

12 Revenue   In the eighteenth century, most government revenue came from tariffs. Administratively, it was the simplest tax to collect. Today this remains true in some developing countries. But in modern economies with sophisticated systems of accounting and administration, it is hard to argue that the administrative costs of raising tax revenue through tariffs are lower than the costs of raising revenue through income taxes or taxes on expenditure.

G. Check your understanding

Read through the text again and make notes on the following:

– how many different kinds of argument the writer lists
– the optimal tariff
– the advantages and disadvantages of such a tariff
– the principle of targeting
– society's way of life
– luxuries
– infant industries

When you have done that, either write a summary of the text or give an oral summary of it.

H. Understanding discourse

Listen to a tutor giving some advice on examinations. Note down the advice.

_____

_____

_____

_____